AF701169

DEPRESSION AND ANXIETY

Simeon Margolis, M.D., Ph.D.

and

Peter V. Rabins, M.D., M.P.H.

ABOUT THE AUTHORS

Simeon Margolis, M.D., Ph.D., received his B.A., M.D., and Ph.D. from Johns Hopkins University and performed his internship and residency at Johns Hopkins Hospital. He is currently a professor of medicine and biological chemistry at the Johns Hopkins School of Medicine and medical editor of *The Johns Hopkins Medical Letter, Health After 50,* as well as a former consultant to the Food and Drug Administration and the National Institutes of Health.

▪ ▪ ▪

Peter V. Rabins, M.D., M.P.H., received his B.A. from the University of Florida, his M.D. from the Tulane University School of Medicine, and his M.P.H. from the Tulane University School of Public Health. He is presently a professor of psychiatry and the director of the Division of Geriatric and Neuropsychiatry at the Johns Hopkins School of Medicine.

1 9 9 6

THIS YEAR'S ADVANCES IN DEPRESSION AND ANXIETY

Research from this year clarifies how depression and anxiety have different effects on individuals and what treatments are most appropriate in each case. For example, one study shows that patients with panic disorder often have symptoms of both depression and anxiety that can affect the type of treatment that these patients receive (see page 39). Furthermore, depression and anxiety have features that are unique in older adults and affect both diagnosis and treatment (see page 34). Other symptoms of depression and anxiety are presented in several case studies, which are new to this White Paper. Also, if you take antidepressant medication, there is a list of practical suggestions to minimize side effects of these drugs on page 25. Other highlights of this year's research include:

- Both genetics and stressful events are known to influence depression, but a new study describes how these two factors might interact. (See page 4.)
- Whether or not depression first strikes at an early age can affect the nature of the disease. (See page 9.)
- Do women suffer greater depression and anxiety than men? (See page 15.)
- As managed health care becomes more common, mental health professionals seek to insure the best treatment for their patients. (See page 17.)
- Many patients with depression do not complete their recommended treatment. (See page 19.)
- Non-drug treatment for depression need not require a psychiatrist. (See page 21.)
- New Prozac side effects were uncovered in a recent study. (See page 30.)
- Relapse of depression can often be treated effectively with the same medication used to successfully treat the first bout of the disease. (See page 32.)
- The social costs of anxiety are outlined in new research. (See page 36.)
- Obsessive-compulsive disorder can be effectively treated with a common antidepressant drug. (See page 40.)
- There is new advice for anxiety patients who are switching medications. (See page 46.)

In addition, you will find the current prices and standard doses of antidepressant and antianxiety drugs beginning on pages 28 and 44, respectively. On pages 49 to 50, there is a bibliography of some of the important articles from the past year. And starting on page 51 is a reprinted article from the *Mayo Clinic Proceedings* that will give you further detail on the detection and treatment of depression and anxiety.

DEPRESSION AND ANXIETY

Depression and anxiety are different, but related, disorders. While their exact pathological cause remains unclear, it is believed that they result from biochemical imbalances in the brain. Depression is thought to occur when there is a defect in the communication between nerve cells (neurons) in the brain. Anxiety disorders may occur from hyperactivity in certain areas of the brain, or may result from decreased activity by the chemical messenger (neurotransmitter) called gamma-amino butyric acid (GABA), which suppresses the action of neurons. Depression is not a sign of weakness or laziness, and anxiety disorders are not the result of a "hypersensitive" or "neurotic" personality. They are bona fide medical disorders, just like diabetes, high blood pressure, and coronary heart disease, and may place an even greater and more devastating burden on afflicted individuals and their families than these other medical conditions.

Depression and anxiety disorders are extremely common. Based on population studies, 8 to 10% of Americans experience a significant mood disorder (usually depression) at some time in their life, and over 4 million Americans suffer from a major depressive illness at any given time. Estimates of the annual costs of depression in the U.S. range from $16 to $45 billion, including the costs of treatment, loss of work productivity, permanent disability, and associated substance abuse. Yet the myths about depression and anxiety persist, even among health professionals. As a result, these disorders are often overlooked, misdiagnosed, or mistreated. One survey found that among patients being treated in outpatient settings for depression, only one-third were taking any medication for their condition. This was true even when such medication was clearly warranted. Of those taking antidepressants, 39% were prescribed smaller doses than generally recommended for treatment. These findings are unfortunate, since proper treatment can be effective. The objective of this paper is to describe depression, mania, and anxiety disorders and to outline and explain the various treatment options.

NEW FINDINGS

The Roles of Genetics and Stress in Depression

Both genetic predisposition and exposure to stressful life events are proven risk factors for depression. A recent study attempted to clarify how genetics and environmental factors might interact to influence a person's risk of major depression.

Researchers interviewed twin sisters (2,164 individuals, average age 30) regarding symptoms of depression and the occurrence of various stressful life events over the past year. A total of 492 episodes of major depression were reported during the year, and four stressful life events were most predictive of the onset of major depression within the month of their occurrence—death of a close relative, assault, serious marital problems, and divorce or break-up of a relationship. Genetic predisposition was also shown to be a strong predictor of major depression. In fact, researchers found that the impact of stressful life events on depression risk is significantly *greater* in those at high genetic risk (that is, when their twin sister has a history of depression) than in those at lower genetic risk. In other words, one way that genetic factors may influence depression risk is by making individuals more sensitive to the depression-inducing impact of stressful life events.

AMERICAN JOURNAL OF PSYCHIATRY
VOLUME 152, NUMBER 6
June 1995

Disorders of Mood: Depression and Mania

Depression and mania are referred to as affective, or mood, disorders. Major hallmarks of depression are a low or sad mood, decreased or absent interest in almost all activities, and a sense of

Anatomy of the Brain

Study of brain function is one of the most active fields in medical research today. While the basic specialized functions of the major components of the brain have long been known, information on how they act together to form emotion is continually being refined. The following is a summary of what is known.

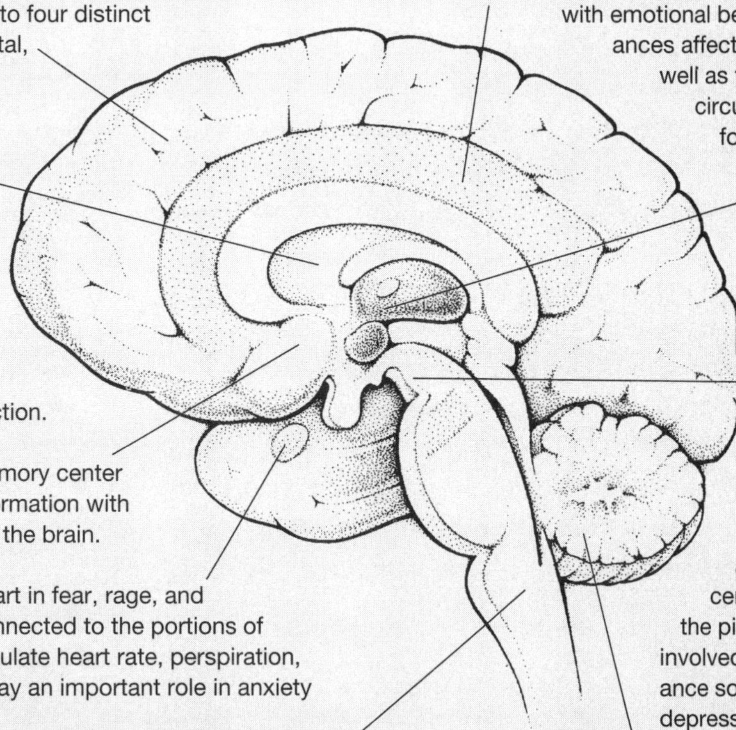

Cerebrum. This outer layer, known as the cerebral cortex, is the center of consciousness, intellect, memory, and language. Each side of the cerebrum is divided into four distinct regions, or lobes (frontal, parietal, occipital, and temporal).

Basal ganglia. A group of complex, interconnected structures that are linked by circuits to the cerebral cortex and the thalamus. Help to initiate thought and action.

Hippocampus. A memory center that matches new information with data already stored in the brain.

Amygdala. Plays a part in fear, rage, and aggression, and is connected to the portions of the brainstem that regulate heart rate, perspiration, and breathing. May play an important role in anxiety disorders.

Brainstem. Links the spinal cord to the higher brain centers, acting as a conduit for the nerves going to and coming from the body. Also manages basic body functions (e.g., breathing, blood pressure).

Limbic system. A ring of structures—including the frontal and temporal lobes of the cerebral cortex, thalamus, hypothalamus, and hippocampus—concerned with emotional behavior. Chemical imbalances affecting the limbic system, as well as the basal ganglia and its circuits, may be responsible for depression and anxiety.

Thalamus. Acts as a relay station where all sensory impulses (but smell) pass on their way to the cerebrum.

Hypothalamus. Aids in controlling body temperature, appetite, water balance, sexual drive, and other body functions; also plays a central part in certain emotions. Regulates the pituitary gland, and may be involved in the hormonal imbalance sometimes associated with depression.

Cerebellum. Controls muscle coordination and balance and plays a role in memory.

worthlessness. Mania is characterized by a heightened mood, increased activity, an overblown self-image, and exaggerated self-confidence. Usually both depression and mania are episodic—that is, bouts of illness are separated by periods of symptomatic recovery. Bipolar illness is a term used to indicate an affective disorder that swings back and forth between depression and mania.

Depression is a particular problem in older people. The National Institute of Mental Health's Epidemiologic Catchment Area Study estimated that of the nation's 31 million people age 65 or older, 1 million suffer from major depression, and an additional 5 million have depressive symptoms that are severe enough to require treatment. In addition, the disease is more often misdiagnosed, and thus left untreated, in the elderly. According to Diagnosis and Treatment of Depression in Late Life, a consensus report from the National Institutes of Health (NIH): "What makes depression in the elderly so insidious is that neither the victim nor the health care provider may recognize its symptoms in the context of the multiple physical problems of many elderly people." Factors that lead to misdiagnosis include: an unwillingness or inability of the elderly to report a low mood; the presence of multiple, chronic medical problems that mask the symptoms of depression; and the social and economic problems that are common in old age. For example, many older persons who live alone have inadequate support mechanisms and are unable to cope with the confusing systems that might provide medical care, social services, or assistance with their funding needs. (See the box on page 34 for more on depression in the elderly.)

CAUSES OF DEPRESSION

Depression was recognized in ancient times. It is described in the Bible and its manifestations are evident among characters in literature. Many famous artists, political leaders, and other public figures have been plagued by the disorder. For example, former first lady Barbara Bush described in her memoirs a six-month bout with depression in 1976.

The specific cause of depression is unknown in most cases. The disorder appears to result from some combination of genetic, psychological, and medical factors. The symptoms of depression are considered primary when they seem to be triggered by some life event (such as the death of a loved one, loss of a job, or pregnancy); they are considered spontaneous when they arise for no apparent reason.

Studies of twins have clearly shown the importance of genetic factors in the development of depression. For example, when one identical twin has an affective disorder, there is a 50 to 90% chance that the other twin will develop the illness at some time. Adopted children whose natural parents had an affective disorder have a three-times-greater incidence of depressive illness than the natural children of their adoptive parents. Genetics also plays a role in treatment. There is some evidence that the son (or any first-degree relative) of a patient whose symptoms respond to a particular antidepressant is himself more likely to respond well to that same drug

NEW RESEARCH

Comparing Depression to Other Chronic Diseases

The negative impact of depression on a patient's perception of his or her health is as great or greater than that of other chronic diseases, according to a recent study of 1,790 persons (average age 55) with either diabetes, hypertension, recent heart attack, congestive heart failure, or depression. At the time of entry into the study and two years later, patients completed questionnaires to assess various aspects of physical and mental health. Their perceptions were scored from 0 to 100, with higher scores representing better health.

Although they had no physical ailments, depressed patients rated their health less favorably than patients with other disorders. They also reported more pain and felt more limited socially by their illness. Those with dysthymia, in particular, reported worse physical functioning than all others except those with congestive heart failure. After two years, depressive symptoms were improved in the depressed patients, however, they still viewed their physical and mental health negatively. These results may simply reflect excessive pessimism among the depressed patients, but they were associated with missed days at work. Thus, though many depressed patients do recover, those with chronic symptoms are more likely to remain persistently disabled to some degree.

ARCHIVES OF GENERAL PSYCHIATRY
VOLUME 52, NUMBER 1
January 1995

Mapping the Brain's Emotional Centers

One of the central questions in brain research today is how different emotions are formed. By pinpointing the mechanisms of normal emotional activity in the brain, scientists hope to gain insight into psychiatric disorders such as depression. A recent study has brought scientists a bit closer to understanding this process.

Using an imaging technique called positron emission tomography (PET), researchers took brain scans of 11 women during moments of happiness, sadness, or a neutral state. In order to induce happiness, the women were told to recall joyful personal experiences, such as a wedding, and were shown pictures of happy faces; to elicit sadness, they concentrated on a sad event, for example a funeral, and were shown sad faces. The PET images recorded changes in regional blood flow during these emotional moments—increased blood flow indicated heightened brain activity and decreased blood flow showed reduced activity—essentially creating a "map" of the brain's emotional centers. Results showed that happiness and sadness involve parts of the limbic system—the ring of structures surrounding the brainstem that has long been considered the center of emotional behavior—but also several areas beyond this system. The following are reproductions of these PET scans, indicating patterns of activity during happiness and sadness.

Happiness (areas of decreased activity)

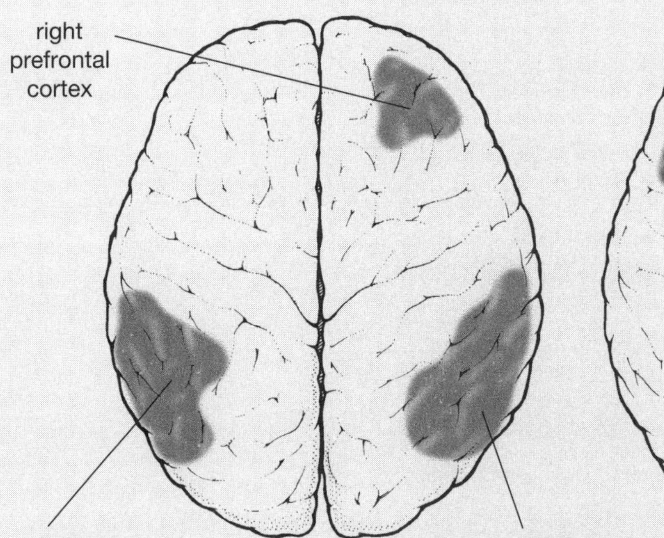

Sadness (areas of increased activity)

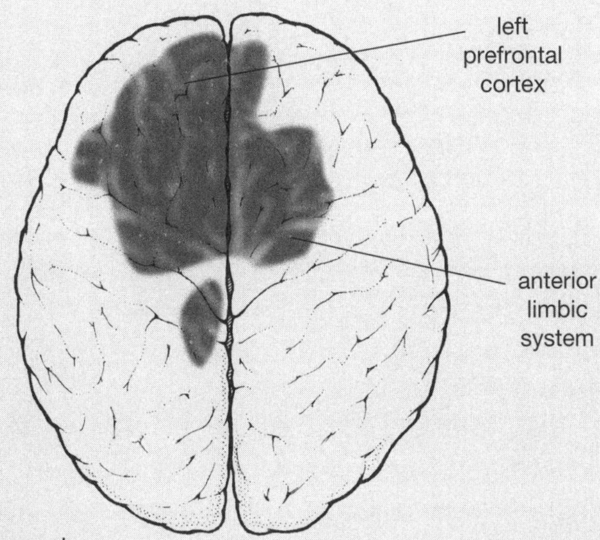

Happiness resulted in decreased activity in the parts of the cerebral cortex involved in forethought and planning.

Sadness was associated with increased activity in parts of the limbic system, including the left prefrontal cortex.

Source: Dr. Mark George, Biological Psychiatry Branch, National Institute of Mental Health.

should he or she become depressed. Still, while hereditary factors may predispose an individual to affective disorders, expression of the illness frequently requires an environmental factor, such as psychological stress. Efforts to identify a specific chromosomal site for a depression gene have given inconsistent results to date.

In about 10 to 15% of cases, affective disorders are secondary to medication, the excessive use of drugs, or neurological or medical abnormalities. Depression can result from the chronic administration of beta blockers, reserpine derivatives, benzodiazepines, cimetidine, or anti-cancer drugs; it can also be precipitated by withdrawal from central nervous system stimulants, like amphetamines or cocaine. Those with dementing brain disorders, such as Alzheimer's disease and Huntington's disease are prone to depression. It can also be a consequence of stroke, affecting about 25% of people who have a stroke in the frontal area of the brain. An underactive or overactive thyroid can lead to the disorder. Adrenal overproduction of cortisol (Cushing's disease) or therapeutic administration of this hormone can cause either depression or mania in some patients. Deficiencies in folic acid, vitamin B_6, or vitamin B_{12} may also cause depression.

Parkinson's disease patients were thought to be at particular risk for depression. However, a recent study found that people with this disorder are no more likely to be depressed than others of similar age and physical disability. After comparing men and women with and without the disease, researchers determined that depression was equally prevalent in both groups. Just 7% of the Parkinson's patients had a mood or anxiety disorder, and only 3% had major depression. Approximately the same number of people in the non-Parkinson's group were affected by these disorders.

A few studies have suggested that reducing blood cholesterol levels can worsen mood and lead to hostile behavior, but a recent five-year study of 233 families suggests that this is not the case. Approximately half of the participants in the study consumed a typical American diet (37% fat calories); the other half ate a cholesterol-lowering diet (low in fat and high in complex carbohydrates). At the end of the study, the typical-diet group experienced an increase in cholesterol levels and a slight lift in mood (as measured by psychological questionnaires). The lowfat-diet group experienced a drop in cholesterol levels and a significantly greater increase in mood, showing improvement in eight out of nine adverse psychological symptoms. The enhanced mood in both groups probably resulted from the experience of participating in a study, where the subjects received a lot of attention from the research team; or, in the case of the lowfat-diet group, knowing that they were doing something to help their health. While this study does not mean that lowering cholesterol levels will improve mood, it does show that eating a cholesterol-lowering diet does not cause depression.

A more recent study provides further detail on the effect of dieting on depression. Researchers surveyed over 2,000 men and women, age 18 to 90, for symptoms of depression as well as their height, weight, physical health, and diet and exercise habits. They found that while being overweight is a risk factor for depression, dieting, rather than carrying extra weight, was the cause. Trying to fit society's image of attractiveness by cutting calories was more stressful than not fitting the image. Perception of poor health was another cause of depression in this group. In sum, these two factors accounted for 92% of the effect of being overweight on depression. Exercise, especially walking, was associated with an improved mood, leading the researchers to comment that "for mental health, the overweight would be best served by increasing their exercise levels rather than dieting, if they want to lose weight."

Depression can also affect the outcome of an illness, as illustrated by the results from a study that followed 222 people who had heart attacks. Researchers found that major depression diagnosed in the hospital was associated with a six-fold increase in the risk of dying from cardiac causes during the following six months. This was the case, even though there was no difference in the severity of coronary heart disease between the depressed and the nondepressed patients. The impact of depression was greatest during this initial period, but the increased risk lasted for at least 18 months after discharge from the hospital. Depression was most common in those patients with a heart rhythm abnormality called premature ventricular contractions. The researchers suggest that depression may cause rhythm changes when the heart muscle is in a weakened state after a heart attack.

Other research has uncovered similar links between depression and cardiovascular disease. One study found that depression increased the risk of events, such as heart attack or stroke, by 59%. Another report found that the presence of depression itself was not linked to cardiovascular disease, but participants whose depression worsened during the course of the study were more likely to suffer a heart attack or stroke or to require surgery to prevent or treat these conditions. These results indicate that depression should be considered a possible warning sign of impending cardiovascular disease.

SYMPTOMS AND DIAGNOSIS

Although severe depression is readily recognized, it can be difficult to distinguish the milder (and more common) forms of depression from the emotional changes that are a part of everyday life. Unlike most medical disorders, depression is not associated with any char-

NEW RESEARCH

Early-Onset vs. Late-Onset Depression

Does a person's age at the time of his or her first depressive episode affect the nature of the depression? In a recent study examining this question, 246 depressed patients (all over age 60) were given a series of questionnaires to determine the frequency of various symptoms—such as guilt, pessimism, anxiety, apathy, and impaired motor coordination. Participants were also assessed for the age of onset of their first depressive episode. Other features, including severity of depression and total number of depressive episodes, were also evaluated.

Only two manifestations of depression differed significantly according to age of onset. Patients who were struck with depression after age 50 had fewer episodes than those whose depression began at a younger age. However, they also had more severe apathy. To explain this disparity, the study's authors cite previous reports linking apathy with structural brain changes, which appear to be a primary cause of first-time depression in older adults (genetics plays a stronger role in early-onset depression). This finding suggests that the onset of low energy or loss of interest in activities formerly enjoyed in older people with no history of depression should not just be attributed to "aging," but should warrant evaluation for possible depression.

AMERICAN JOURNAL OF PSYCHIATRY
VOLUME 152, NUMBER 5
May 1995

Identifying Depression

Primary care doctors use a number of different questionnaires to screen their patients for symptoms of depression. Reproduced below is one of the most commonly used: The Center for Epidemiologic Studies Depression Scale (CES-D). The CES-D has proven to be a valuable tool for detecting possible cases of major depression or a milder mood disorder; but people who test positive are not necessarily depressed. A definitive diagnosis can only be made after a clinical interview with a doctor. For an accurate result, complete every question, add up your total score, and then read the scoring key below.

During the past week	**Rarely or none of the time (less than 1 day)**	**Some or a little of the time (1 to 2 days)**	**Occasionally or a moderate amount of the time (3 to 4 days)**	**Most or all of the time (5 to 7 days)**
1. I was bothered by things that don't usually bother me.	0	1	2	3
2. I did not feel like eating; my appetite was poor.	0	1	2	3
3. I felt that I could not shake off the blues, even with the help of my family or friends.	0	1	2	3
4. I felt that I was just as good as other people.	3	2	1	0
5. I had trouble keeping my mind on what I was doing.	0	1	2	3
6. I felt depressed.	0	1	2	3
7. I felt everything I did was an effort.	0	1	2	3
8. I felt hopeful about the future.	3	2	1	0
9. I thought my life had been a failure.	0	1	2	3
10. I felt fearful.	0	1	2	3
11. My sleep was restless.	0	1	2	3
12. I was happy.	3	2	1	0
13. I talked less than usual.	0	1	2	3
14. I felt lonely.	0	1	2	3
15. People were unfriendly.	0	1	2	3
16. I enjoyed life.	3	2	1	0
17. I had crying spells.	0	1	2	3
18. I felt sad.	0	1	2	3
19. I felt that people disliked me.	0	1	2	3
20. I could not get "going."	0	1	2	3

Scoring: A score of 22 or higher indicates depression; if you score within this range, consult a doctor for a definitive diagnosis.

Source: L.S. Radloff, "The CES-D Scale: A Self-Report Depression Scale for Research in the General Population." *Applied Psychological Measurement* 1 (1977): 385-401.

acteristic laboratory changes or microscopic tissue abnormalities that can be used to confirm a suspected diagnosis. The American Psychiatric Association has established diagnostic classification systems that allow consistent diagnoses of major depression, mania, and the various forms of anxiety. These criteria are contained in the revised fourth edition of the *Diagnostic and Statistical Manual of Mental Disorders* (DSM-IVR).

Major Depression

According to the DSM-IVR, a person is suffering a major depressive episode if he or she exhibits four or more of the following symptoms continually for more than two weeks:

- depressed mood with overwhelming feelings of sadness and grief
- loss of interest and pleasure in activities formerly enjoyed
- insomnia, early-morning waking, or oversleeping nearly every day
- decreased energy; fatigue
- noticeable changes in appetite and weight (significant loss or gain)
- feelings of guilt, worthlessness, and helplessness
- inability to concentrate or think; indecisiveness
- recurrent thoughts of death and suicide; suicide attempts
- physical symptoms of restlessness or being slowed down.

The diagnosis is more secure when these criteria are supplemented by either a positive family history, a prior episode of depression or mania, or the presence of a precipitating factor, such as a recent stroke or the use of medications known to cause mood disorders. Additional symptoms of depression include disorganized thinking, delusions, decreased sexual drive, and constipation. In most cases, the symptoms of major depression include abnormalities in both cognitive (thinking) and bodily functions, as well as disturbances in mood.

Episodes of major depression range from mild to severe. In mild episodes the symptoms barely meet the minimum requirements for the diagnosis and the associated functional impairment is minor. Severe episodes are characterized by several excessive symptoms and marked interference with social and job-related functions. Severely afflicted individuals have difficulty doing almost any activity—going to work, socializing with friends, or even simply getting up in the morning. They may be unable to feed and clothe themselves, or maintain personal hygiene.

Suicide. Suicide, the tenth leading cause of death in the U.S., is a major complication of depression. Some 50 to 70% of suicides in the U.S. are due to depression, and about 15% of severely de-

NEW RESEARCH

The Effect of Depression on Mental Function

In older adults, depression has an important impact on cognition (one's thinking processes, such as judgment, reasoning, and memory), according to a recent study. Researchers assessed the cognitive abilities of 220 patients (average age 76) who were entering an acute care program for such conditions as orthopedic injury, stroke, and diabetes. Depression, dementia, and memory were measured in each patient using standardized tests.

Some 30% of the subjects scored above the cutoff point for depression. In these patients, cognition scores worsened as the level of depression rose. Overall, a patient's depression score accounted for approximately 8% of his or her cognition rating. Age is another factor that has a major effect on cognition. As the researchers conclude: "Depression in the elderly cannot be dismissed as unimportant or irrelevant to functional outcome." In other words, treating depression can improve cognitive function of older people. Other studies have found that both depression and cognition are important in predicting which patients will recover from strokes and orthopedic injuries.

JOURNAL OF GERONTOLOGY
VOLUME 508, NUMBER 1
January 1995

CASE STUDY: MAJOR DEPRESSION

A 66-year-old executive consulted a psychiatrist about a three-month feeling of tiredness, declining interest in work, and constant worry. She had undergone a cardiac surgery five years ago and recently began worrying that she might need another operation. Despite her physician's reassurance that she was doing well, her worries would not subside. In addition to persistent unfounded worry, she reported difficulty falling asleep and frequent awakening through the night. She felt that she was becoming inept at work, and was considering retirement. Treatment for depression was initiated, and within six weeks both the patient and her husband reported that she was back to her usual self. She felt that her efficiency at her job had improved, and she was once again enjoying her work.

pressed people commit suicide. In one Swedish study, the number of suicides among patients with affective disorders was about 80 times higher than in the general population and eight times greater than in those with other psychiatric disorders. The risk of suicide is highest among white males and among those who live alone, have made prior suicide attempts, refuse psychiatric evaluation, or abuse alcohol or drugs. Although women attempt suicide three to four times more often than men, men are three to four times more successful in their suicide efforts.

In addition to the symptoms of major depression, there are warning signs to look for in severely depressed individuals who may try to commit suicide. Unfortunately, it is impossible to predict accurately who will make such an attempt. Although many risk factors are identifiable, not all people who commit suicide have these risk factors, and most people who do have them are not suicidal. All too often, however, friends and family of people who commit suicide are unaware of the following warning signs until it is too late.

- social isolation that may be self-imposed
- drastic mood swings or overall personality changes
- neglecting home, finances, pets
- exaggerated complaints of aches or pains
- recent psychological trauma, such as a divorce, death of a loved one, or job loss (These crises may trigger suicidal thinking in an already depressed person.)
- giving away cherished belongings to loved ones; putting one's affairs in order
- sudden calm or cheerfulness after a period of depression
- frequent use of alcohol or other drugs
- buying a gun

• verbal threats of suicide or statements that suggest a desire to die
• family history of suicide or previous suicide attempts.

Dysthymia

This condition, also called depressive neurosis, is characterized by the presence of mild depression for at least two years. Dysthymia is twice as common in women as in men. The condition may be intermittent, with periods of normal feelings, but relief never lasts beyond two months. About 10% of people with dysthymia also have intermittent episodes of major depression, a condition named double-depression. Symptoms that accompany dysthymia during depressive phases include:

• feelings of worthlessness, low self-esteem
• noticeable changes in appetite and weight (significant loss or gain)
• noticeable changes in sleeping patterns (such as insomnia, early-morning waking, or oversleeping)
• decreased energy, fatigue
• inability to concentrate or think; indecisiveness
• persistent feelings of hopelessness.

Bipolar Disorder

The combination of major depressive episodes and mania are used to make the diagnosis of bipolar disorder. Manic episodes are characterized by a distinct period of abnormally and persistently elevated, expansive, or irritable mood. The episodes are severe enough to affect usual functioning at work and/or at home. Episodes with milder manic symptoms have been termed hypomania. Bipolar disorders occur slightly more often in women than in men. Men tend to have more manic episodes, however, while depressive episodes are more common among women.

The illness can start with either a depressive or manic bout, but about two-thirds start with a manic episode, and mania tends to predominate. A manic episode is accompanied by at least three of the following symptoms:

• feelings of grandeur or inflated self-esteem
• diminished need for sleep
• being extremely talkative
• sensing that thoughts and ideas are racing
• being easily distracted
• increased productivity/activity at work, at school, or in social situations
• excessive involvement in high-risk activities that are likely to have

painful consequences (such as extramarital affairs or unsound business deals).

During manic episodes, individuals must be protected from engaging in self-destructive actions such as making terrible investments or other foolish business decisions, giving their money away, going on large spending sprees, driving recklessly, or committing sexual indiscretions.

Seasonal Affective Disorder (SAD)

Some people experience episodes of depression only during certain seasons of the year—usually the winter months, hence the name winter depression or seasonal affective disorder (SAD). Typically, the symptoms of depression begin in the fall, worsen in the winter, and improve in the spring. Some patients with this type of illness can be successfully treated with exposure to bright white light. Light therapy generally involves sitting for at least one hour a day in front of banks of fluorescent lights. Improvement may begin within a few days, and symptoms often disappear after two to three weeks of light treatment; continued exposure to bright light is needed, however, to prevent a relapse. Although commercially available light boxes are advertised as providing benefits for depressed people, these devices are not approved by the Food and Drug Administration; light therapy should be tried only under professional supervision.

Beta blockers may eventually offer a second form of treatment for SAD. One study published in the fall of 1994 found that 73% of SAD patients responded favorably to morning doses (between 5:30 and 6:00 a.m.) of the beta blocker propranolol. These patients achieved significantly better scores on a scale indicating depressive symptoms than patients taking a placebo (dummy pill). Beta blockers may work by suppressing the increased melatonin production that is associated with the longer periods of darkness during winter.

Grief vs. Depression

The loss of a loved one can cause intense and unique emotions. This experience can certainly be a trigger for a major depressive episode, but few people in mourning experience true depression. Grief may produce a wide range of feelings, and the grieving process can be lengthy or short. Current research suggests that the "success" of grieving should not be measured by the process, but by the griever's acceptance of the loss. Also, the end of the grieving process is not marked by the end of sadness—deep sadness over a death may well last a lifetime. Grieving ends when the sadness becomes integrated into the mourner's sense of self. A good sign that mourning is becoming complete is a shift to positive and realistic plans for the future. As this gradual shift happens—and the mourner enjoys life more than being weighed down by it—the work of grieving becomes complete.

One might suspect that mourning has been unsuccessful—and seek the help of a physician or another health professional—if the following symptoms are present for a prolonged period of time, or if they arise months or even years after the loss:

- physical symptoms that mimic the illness or injury of the person who died
- overuse of alcohol or drugs
- persistent depression
- chronic sleep difficulties
- thoughts of or attempts at suicide (see a health professional immediately if this occurs)
- inability to carry out normal daily routines.

It is important to seek medical help for physical symptoms that arise during mourning, as well as to attend to conditions that existed prior to the loss. Some evidence suggests that acute mourning may suppress the immune system, making mourners more susceptible to illness.

NATURAL HISTORY AND PROGNOSIS OF DEPRESSION

Affective disorders most often surface between ages 20 and 30, but they can occur at any age. The duration of an untreated episode of major depression is usually eight to nine months. This period can be shortened considerably with proper diagnosis and treatment. On average, two-thirds of those who recover completely from an acute episode have recurrent bouts of either depression or mania. Half of these recurrences tend to be manic, even in people whose first episode is depression. Bipolar disorder usually begins at an earlier age and has more recurrences. The median number of recurrences is four; episodes can be separated by weeks, months, or often by years. Over time, however, the recurrences tend to become more frequent. One subgroup of patients with bipolar disorder can cycle between depressive and manic episodes as often as four times a year. Those with double-depression are more likely to experience chronic depression or have more bouts of major depression.

NEW RESEARCH

Distress and Gender

Women are believed to suffer greater levels of distress—depression, agitation, anxiety, and malaise—because they report more symptoms on psychological tests, but does this reflect a greater incidence of these disorders in women or a greater ease in disclosing emotions? Men, on the other hand, are considered more likely to express anger. Both of these assumptions were examined in a recent study by analyzing the frequency of feelings such as sadness, happiness, anxiety, and anger in 1,282 women and 749 men over a week's time.

Results showed that women do indeed express emotions more freely than men. Even after accounting for this factor, however, women were still 30% more likely to be depressed and anxious than men. Furthermore, women overall were found to be as angry or angrier than men. For example, a woman is more likely to escalate from simple anger to yelling than an equally-angry man. The study's authors concluded that women do not just express emotion differently, but "genuinely suffer more distress than men." The reasons for this remain to be discovered.

AMERICAN SOCIOLOGICAL REVIEW
VOLUME 60, NUMBER 3
June 1995

CASE STUDY: STROKE-INDUCED DEPRESSION

A 71-year-old woman was diagnosed by mammogram as possibly having breast cancer. She decided to forego a biopsy or any further evaluation, stating, "I don't feel very well and I'd rather not prolong things." Her physician became concerned about depression and referred her to a psychiatrist for assessment. To the psychiatrist, the patient admitted she had not felt her usual energetic, optimistic self for almost four years since suffering a minor stroke. Although she had fully recovered from the stroke, she felt "this was the beginning of the end." The biggest change reported by her husband was that she had always been a high-spirited person who had been undaunted by many stresses during her life. In spite of her absolute conviction that all of her problems related to "old age," she agreed to treatment with counseling and medication.

Soon after treatment was initiated, the patient reported sleeping and eating better, and within three weeks, her energy improved. Six weeks after treatment began she spontaneously called her primary physician and said "I've reconsidered." She could never explain her initial pessimism, but now wanted a definitive answer to her problem. When the biopsy tested positive for breast cancer, she agreed to radiation therapy and anti-estrogen medication for her cancer. Two years later, she remained well and convinced that she had made "the right choice."

Alcoholism also affects recovery from depression. In a recent study, researchers tracked 176 men and women who fit the criteria for both alcoholism and major depression and 412 people with major depression alone. Those who were never alcoholics or were non-active alcoholics were twice as likely to recover from an episode of major depression than subjects who were active alcoholics. However, active alcoholism did not increase the chance of having recurrent major depressive episodes, suggesting that depression is triggered by other factors. Although active alcoholism may not cause depression, it makes recovery more difficult if depression occurs.

TREATMENT OF DEPRESSION AND MANIA

Depression and mania respond well to treatment. In about 80% of cases, proper diagnosis and treatment of these disorders leads to a complete remission. The four options for dealing with depression and mania are: antidepressant medications; psychotherapy; other treatments, such as electroconvulsive therapy or light therapy; or any combination of these. Starting treatment as early as possible is important, since depression becomes more difficult to treat the longer it lasts. Response to any particular treatment varies among patients, so a person who does not respond to the first type tried is likely to respond to a different one. Medications are probably the most common form of therapy, and any given antidepressant drug has a 70% chance of working.

Psychotherapy alone helps more than half of mildly to moderately depressed persons. The more severe cases of depression are best treated with medication. Up to 80% of severely depressed patients improve with electroconvulsive therapy (which is only used in particular cases).

Combination therapy is rarely necessary for initial treatment of uncomplicated, nonchronic depression. However, using psychotherapy in conjunction with medication may be beneficial if either treatment alone produces only partial results; if the depression is chronic; or if an evaluation suggests discrete aspects of a disorder that are best treated by different means, such as medication for depressive symptoms and psychotherapy for job-related problems.

Treating depression has three goals. In order of importance, they are: to lessen the symptoms of depression (for example, depressed mood, insomnia, inability to concentrate); to return patients to their previous ability to function socially and in the workplace; and to reduce the likelihood of a recurrence. The goals for mania are somewhat different because it is more difficult to treat. They are, as recently described by the American Psychiatric Association's "Practice Guideline for the Treatment of Patients with Bipolar Disorder," to reduce the frequency and severity of episodes, as well as their social and psychological impact, and to improve the patient's ability to function socially and mentally in-between episodes.

Treatment goals are accomplished over three stages: acute, continuation, and maintenance. Acute treatment focuses on immediate relief from symptoms and restoration of function. Once symptoms start responding to acute treatment, continuation treatment is begun to prevent any relapse. If a patient is without symptoms for four to nine months after an episode, he or she is considered recovered. At this point, maintenance treatment is initiated to prevent the occurrence of a new episode; it can last for one year to a lifetime, depending on the individual. Depression recurs in about half of cases within two years after stopping treatment.

Finding a Therapist

Concern over possible symptoms of depression or mania does not mean that a person must seek help from a psychiatrist who is a complete stranger. The majority of patients with depression are treated

NEW RECOMMENDATION

Managed Health Care and the Treatment of Depression

Mental health professionals have expressed concern over how managed health care plans, which rely on primary care physicians to treat a broad variety of conditions, can provide effective care in the more specialized area of mental health. A recent study found that alternating visits between a primary care physician and a psychiatrist may be best for some patients in a managed care setting.

The study followed 217 patients, age 19 to 80, with minor or major depression. Subjects were treated either by a primary care physician alone (usual care) or they alternated between a primary care physician and a psychiatrist who educated them about depression and antidepressants; discussed life events; and adjusted medication for some (collaborative care). Most patients in both groups were treated with tricyclic drugs.

During the seven-month follow-up period, patients with major depression did best with collaborative care: By one symptom scale, 74% of these patients improved their scores by half, compared to only 44% of usual care patients. Collaborative care also improved adherence to treatment for both major and minor depression patients. However, those with minor depression improved equally well with either style of care, and may only need to see a primary care physician.

JOURNAL OF THE AMERICAN MEDICAL ASSOCIATION
VOLUME 273, NUMBER 13
April 5, 1995

CASE STUDY: DEPRESSION WITH APATHY

An 82-year-old woman was referred for evaluation of a 25 pound weight loss. A full medical assessment revealed no identifiable cause. Her primary physician had been concerned for several months that she was depressed, but the patient had adamantly denied this and refused to be treated for depression. However, she ultimately agreed to be seen by a psychiatrist, "since they can't find anything." She told the psychiatrist that she had always enjoyed eating and that her weight had been "a bit of a problem" in the past. In fact, she "rather enjoyed" the weight she had lost, although she realized that she had also lost all pleasure in eating and missed her previous enjoyment relating to food.

When asked directly, she also said that she had become less interested in her grandchildren and in reading, "the two most important passions of my life." These changes were very distressing to her, but she could not explain them except to say: "Maybe that's what happens when you get old." She denied any feelings of sadness or depression. Based on the lack of pleasure she was getting from usual activities, her significant loss of appetite, and her diminished energy, the psychiatrist diagnosed depression. After two months of counseling were ineffective, an antidepressant medication was begun and improvement was noted within three months.

by their family physician. By starting with a primary care physician, other medical conditions that could be responsible for the symptoms can be ruled out. If the diagnosis is depression, the primary care physician can initiate drug therapy and/or coordinate care from other specialists.

Many different kinds of mental health professionals are available—psychiatrists, psychologists, psychotherapists, nurse specialists, and social workers. Choosing the type of therapy that is best for an individual depends on the severity of the symptoms and the cost of treatment, among other factors. No matter what type of therapy is selected, however, searching for the right therapist may take some research. A family physician will be able to provide some recommendations, but there are other sources as well. Local medical societies, university medical centers, and national mental health organizations may be able to provide assistance. Also check community mental health clinics, local schools, and religious organizations, which sometimes offer inexpensive or even free counseling programs.

Compatibility is an extremely important factor, and it may take more than one referral to find a comfortable counseling relationship. In addition, it is important to ask about a therapist's education and professional licenses, either before making an appointment or face to face. A patient can get a feel for a therapist by describing his or her condition and asking the therapist how he or she would resolve it. Reputable practitioners will not object to requests for information about their background, and will understand the need to interview with another therapist.

Psychiatrists. These medical doctors have several years of postgraduate training in the diagnosis and treatment of mental or emotional disorders. Psychiatrists can prescribe medications and hospitalize patients, and are often consulted in complex cases, especially when medical complications are also present.

Psychologists. Clinical psychologists have a doctoral degree (Ph.D. or Psy.D.) in psychology and are trained in counseling, psychotherapy, and psychological testing. Most states in the U.S. require psychologists to have postdoctoral training in addition to the doctoral degree.

Psychotherapists. Mental health professionals do not need any training or a license to practice as psychotherapists. Be certain to ask the practitioner about his/her qualifications before entering into therapy.

Psychiatric social workers. These professionals make up the largest segment of the mental health field. Licensing requirements differ from state to state. A social worker with a master's degree often has specialized training in counseling.

Psychiatric nurse specialists. These registered nurses usually hold a master's degree in psychiatric nursing and specialize in treating mental or psychiatric disorders. They often conduct therapy in a hospital setting.

Psychotherapy

Psychotherapy is the treatment of an emotional, behavioral, personality, or psychiatric disorder by means of verbal and nonverbal communication, as opposed to the use of medication or physical interventions. Like any medical treatment, it has advantages and disadvantages. Used on its own, psychotherapy produces no physiologic side effects—an especially important consideration for older adults, who use prescription drugs approximately three times more often than the general population and are therefore at greater risk for adverse interactions with antidepressants. Psychotherapy may also help patients learn to cope with or avoid factors contributing to a recurrence of depression, and offers the possibility of effective treatment for patients who tried drugs, but did not respond to them. However, it may take longer to achieve any benefit using psychotherapy: six to eight weeks, as compared to four to six weeks for

NEW RESEARCH

Complying with Depression Treatment Guidelines

Guidelines from the Agency for Health Care Policy and Research describe effective treatment measures for depression, but ensuring that patients will comply with them is problematic. One study followed 91 primary care patients given the antidepressant nortriptyline (Pamelor) for major depression, and found that only 55% of them completed the acute phase of treatment (in which symptoms are brought under control). After six months, just 33% of them had finished the recommended regimen, which included relapse prevention.

As the researchers note, compliance can be difficult with most diseases. Some 50% of hypertension patients, for example, fail to keep follow-up appointments, and 40% of them do not take medications as prescribed. Although some patients in this study dropped out because they did not respond to the drug, others may have done so out of dissatisfaction with the form of treatment. In particular, 13 patients did not even appear for their first drug therapy visit: Many of them had expressed preference for psychotherapy instead of medication.

These results underscore the need for patient education concerning the importance of finishing treatment, as well as the need for patients to participate in selecting a treatment method (as the AHCPR guidelines recommend) in order to improve compliance.

ARCHIVES OF FAMILY MEDICINE
VOLUME 4, NUMBER 2
February 1995

medication. Also, psychotherapy alone may not be effective in patients with severe depression, and sessions are time-consuming and may be inconvenient.

Based on the severity of the illness and factors specific for each patient, therapists select a combination of different approaches from the range of psychotherapeutic techniques described below. Essential to all psychotherapy is the establishment of a trusting relationship with the therapist that enables the patient to share confidences, life experiences, and problems. As a result, medication is generally more appropriate in patients who are unable to communicate because depression has caused severe physical debilitation or they are suffering from delusions.

Interpersonal therapy. Also known as crisis intervention, this approach focuses on the relationship between the patient and his/her current life situation. Depressive symptoms are assumed to be due to environmental stressors, such as divorce, difficult transitions, and unfulfilling personal relationships. The therapist helps the patient resolve conflicts and restore the balance in life through awareness and, possibly, behavior modification. The goal is to help the patient cope with the immediate problem. This approach is most effective when depression is due to a life event, such as the death of a spouse.

Psychodynamic therapy. This is the most common form of psychotherapy. It may focus on one's previous experiences in an attempt to understand present-day conflicts or emphasize feelings about recent changes, such as retirement or grief. This therapy attempts to treat the "whole person," rather than just the symptoms of depression. A crucial element of the therapy is "transference," when the patient transfers feelings about important childhood figures onto the therapist, who then works to help the patient resolve residual/past conflicts. This therapy can be effective in helping a patient overcome destructive personality patterns.

Supportive therapy. In supportive therapy, patients are provided with knowledge and feedback concerning their diagnosis, probable causes of their illness, rationale for treatment, and prognosis. It is an adjunctive therapy that complements more effective treatment. The therapist can bolster patient morale by exhibiting an optimistic attitude and persistently emphasizing the good prospects for curing the depression. Support and education are extended to the patient's family and any close friends who may be enlisted to help. Other features of supportive therapy include: guiding the patient with regard to work and interpersonal relationships; helping the patient set tangible and realistic goals; discouraging the initiation of major decisions or lifestyle changes that may be prompted by the patient's depressed state; and remaining alert to the side effects of drugs, improvements in mood, and the appearance of suicidal impulses.

Behavioral therapy. This type of therapy is based on the premise that depressed patients adopt abnormal behaviors that prolong their depression, and that these behaviors are learned and reinforced in the environment. Training is provided to improve social skills, problem solving, scheduling of activities, and self-control. Behavioral therapy emphasizes day-to-day improvements in behavior, and is most often effective when the problem is clearly defined. Self-reward after "good" behavior is encouraged. While of unproven benefit in the treatment of depression, behavioral therapy has been useful in relieving some of the complications of depression, such as obsessive-compulsive disorder and phobias (see pages 40 and 41).

Cognitive therapy. The aim of cognitive therapy is to reverse the patient's belief that exaggerated weaknesses and inadequacies doom him or her to inevitable failure in the future. The therapist not only encourages the patient to recognize that these views are distorted, but also attempts to bolster confidence by demonstrating that the patient can successfully complete increasingly complex assignments. The treatment generally requires 20 sessions, over 10 to 20 weeks, and is often combined with behavioral therapy.

Psychoanalytic therapy. The psychoanalytic theory of depression derives from the Freudian concept that the altered mood develops due to anger directed towards oneself. The theory further asserts that cure of the depression requires that the cause of the anger be exposed and dealt with in a realistic manner. The patient meets three to five times a week with the therapist in a stream-of-consciousness, free-association atmosphere that involves minimal feedback from the therapist. Because classical psychoanalysis requires years of treatment, it is not suitable for the treatment of acute depression. In any event, this method is rarely used in its pure form today, although aspects of the Freudian approach have survived under psychodynamic therapy.

Group therapy. In this method, a number of people meet together and discuss problems under the guidance of a therapist. Participants can share personal feelings, experiences, and solutions in a supportive atmosphere. The resulting interaction often works to lessen feelings of isolation on the part of the individual and can

NEW FINDINGS

Treating Depression with Problem Solving Therapy

Problem solving therapy is as effective as antidepressant medication for patients suffering from major depression, according to a new study involving 91 patients seeing their primary care doctor. Each patient was randomly assigned to receive either a placebo, the tricyclic antidepressant amitriptyline (Elavil, Endep), or problem solving therapy over a 12-week period. Problem solving (a variation of behavioral therapy) is based on the premise that emotional symptoms are created by difficulties in dealing with problems in daily life. The therapy improves depressive symptoms by identifying the patient's life problems and working to solve them one at a time. Therapy sessions took place every other week.

After 12 weeks, 60% of the patients assigned to problem solving therapy were considered recovered from their depression, compared to 52% of those taking amitriptyline and 27% of those given a placebo. All of the 28 patients completing the problem solving therapy rated it as helpful or very helpful, compared to 21 of the 25 patients on amitriptyline. This study also demonstrates that, in certain specific cases, effective and satisfying non-drug treatment can be given by a primary care physician without necessarily requiring a psychiatrist.

BRITISH MEDICAL JOURNAL
VOLUME 310, NUMBER 6977
February 18, 1995

heighten awareness and understanding of one's own problems. It is useful for people who need feedback from peers.

If psychotherapy alone produces no response by six weeks or only a partial response by 12 weeks, medication may be the next best step, given its effectiveness. There is currently insufficient research to say definitively whether or not continuing psychotherapy after adding medication will be beneficial, so the therapist and patient will have to determine what would be best.

Drug Treatment

The current antidepressant drugs were introduced in essentially two waves. Tricyclics, such as imipramine (Tipramine, Tofranil), were first used in the mid-1950s, along with monoamine oxidase (MAO) inhibitors, such as iproniazid. In the late 1980s, fluoxetine (Prozac) was developed along with a handful of similar drugs called selective serotonin reuptake inhibitors (SSRIs). Today, physicians can choose from a growing number of medications. These include tetracyclics, such as maprotiline (Ludiomil), and dopamine reuptake inhibitors, such as bupropion (Wellbutrin), in addition to tricyclics, MAO inhibitors, and SSRIs. Antimanic drugs, like lithium (Eskalith, Lithobid) and valproate (Depakene, Depakote), treat bipolar disorders and prevent relapse. Acute mania is sometimes treated with neuroleptic medications, such as haloperidol (Haldol).

There are several advantages to treating depression with medications: they are effective against mild, moderate, and severe forms of major depression; patients usually respond more quickly to drugs than psychotherapy (as much as two weeks sooner); they are easy to administer; and they require little time from the patient. In addition, patients should be assured that antidepressants are not addictive and, when properly administered, are rarely dangerous. However, drug treatment can cause unwanted side effects; it requires strict adherence to a medication schedule and repeated medical visits to monitor response; and many patients (10 to 30%) fail to complete treatment. Older individuals and those with chronic illness are more susceptible to the adverse effects of antidepressants.

Although researchers know that these drugs work by affecting levels of neurotransmitters (chemical messengers that communicate between individual nerve cells) in the brain, they cannot determine which medication will be most effective in any particular individual. Therefore, drug selection remains largely a process of educated guesses, though typically, about 60% of patients have

NEW FINDINGS

Treating Depression and Alcoholism

Although depression and alcoholism are a dangerous combination, several studies have shown that treatment brings rapid relief. In a new five-year study, researchers compared three groups of patients: depressed alcoholics; nondepressed alcoholics; and depressed patients who were not alcoholics. They found that the depressed alcoholic patients had more severe suicidal symptoms (death wishes, thoughts of suicide, suicidal behavior) and lower self-esteem than the depressed patients without an alcohol problem. In addition, the depressed alcoholic patients were significantly more impaired in their ability to function at work, within the family, and in adapting to new situations, compared to the non-alcoholic depressed patients. The study also showed that among alcoholics, depression interfered with sleep and decreased libido.

Because of the unique effects that depression and alcoholism have on each other, concurrence of the two disorders may warrant treatment in a hospital that specializes in both. Fortunately, hospitalization is often relatively brief for these patients, with substantial improvement within a few weeks of admission, despite the severity of initial symptoms.

AMERICAN JOURNAL OF PSYCHIATRY
VOLUME 152, NUMBER 3
March 1995

Effectiveness of Antidepressant Therapy

People are generally less accepting of psychiatric treatments than other types of medical interventions. But according to a recent report commissioned by the National Institute of Mental Health, the effectiveness of treatment with a single antidepressant drug compares favorably to balloon angioplasty, a common treatment for coronary heart disease in which a small balloon is inflated inside a blocked coronary artery to create a wider path for blood flow. As the data shown below indicate, single-drug antidepressant therapy is at least as effective, if not more so, than angioplasty.

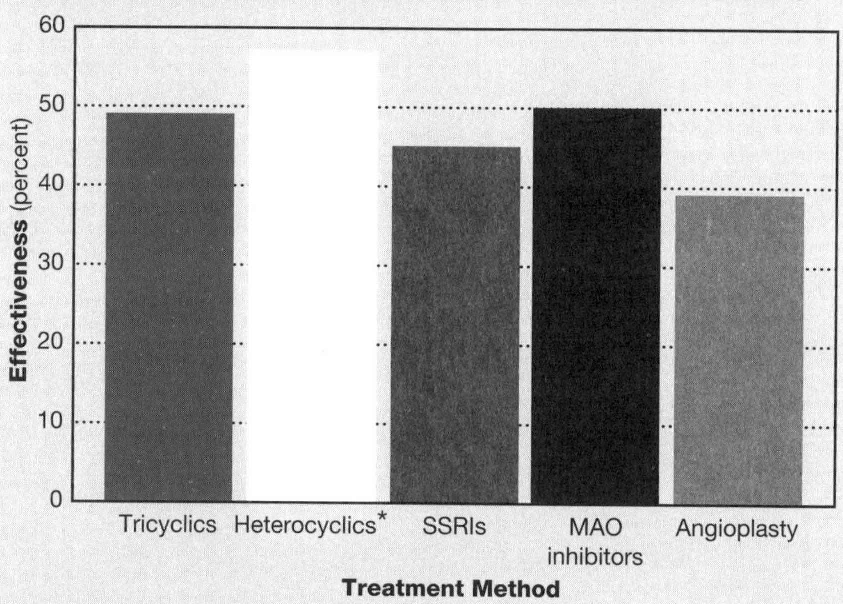

*Amoxapine, bupropion, maprotiline, trazodone.
Source: *Psychopharmacology Bulletin,* 1993.

some response to the first antidepressant they try. For first-time patients with moderate to severe depression and no other mental symptoms or general medical conditions, the choice of medication is generally based on avoidance of side effects. For example, amitriptyline (Elavil) can lower blood pressure and cause sedation and confusion—side effects that are especially troublesome for older individuals. Family history can also determine which drug would be most effective. If a first-degree relative (for example, a father or sister) responds well to one medication, a drug from the same class may be an appropriate first choice. This also holds true for side effects: The response of a first-degree relative may indicate the patient's response as well.

By themselves, antidepressant drugs usually produce a significant improvement within six weeks. If the depression is responding fully to medication after this period, treatment moves on to the continuation phase (see page 17), which lasts for four to nine months at the same level of dosage. Patients who still show some impairment after six weeks should be reassessed after an additional six weeks (many are likely to improve further during this time). Their physician may then adjust the medication dosage to improve response.

When a drug fails to produce results after six weeks, or only produces partial results after eight to 12 weeks, a new one may be tried. The new drug would probably be selected from a different class of medications, since drugs in the same class tend to work similarly. In 20 to 50% of patients, it can be helpful to augment the action of an antidepressant by adding another drug, such as lithium. However, this increases the risk of side effects and adverse drug interactions. If a drug from one class is producing good results, but its side effects are unacceptable, changing to a different drug from the same class may reduce the adverse effects. In some cases, blood levels of the antidepressant are followed to monitor patients at risk of developing toxic levels of the drug. These include older patients and those with other serious physical disorders. If maintenance treatment is not required, drugs are withdrawn slowly over a period of three to four weeks. Relapses are most common during the first two months after stopping an antidepressant.

Antidepressants must be prescribed with caution in depressed individuals who are suicidal. Suicidal thoughts or attempts are common symptoms of depression, and the risk of suicide is thought to increase as the depression begins to respond to treatment; as depression lessens, patients might begin to regain just enough energy and motivation to actually consider following through on a suicidal urge. Antidepressants are the fourth leading cause of drug overdose and the third leading cause of drug-related death. Tricyclics are the most common cause of death from overdose with an antidepressant.

Tricyclics. Named for their chemical structure—a chain of three rings—these drugs raise brain concentrations of the neurotransmitters norepinephrine and serotonin by blocking their reabsorption by the nerve cells (neurons) that release them. A puzzling feature of tricyclics is that their effect on neurotransmitters is rapid, but it takes weeks before depression improves. The tricyclics are the drugs of choice for the treatment of moderate to severe depression. They have not proven effective for chronic low-grade depression or dysthymia, and they are rarely used for the management of temporary depressions arising from difficult life situations, such as the loss of a spouse. About 60% of tricyclic users experience significant improvement over the course of four to six

Minimizing the Side Effects of Antidepressants

The benefits of antidepressant drugs may often be offset by unpleasant side effects. If these symptoms are severe enough to interfere with daily functions, discuss the situation with your doctor. He or she may be able to suggest a solution, such as decreasing the dosage or trying a new drug. In many cases, side effects will fade or become less noticeable over time. The following are practical suggestions for patients to minimize common antidepressant side effects. Consult your doctor before making any changes in your medication regimen.

Tricyclic Antidepressants and Maprotiline

Constipation. Drink at least eight glasses of water or juice every day and add foods high in fiber—such as wheat bran, beans, or whole grain cereal—to your diet. Talk to your doctor about trying bulk laxatives, stool softeners, or fiber-containing products.

Dizziness upon standing. Stand up slowly after sitting or lying down, and wait 30 seconds before trying to walk.

Drowsiness. Take the medication—in one dose, if possible—30 minutes before bed time to minimize sleepiness during the day.*

Dry mouth. Try chewing on sugarless gum or candy. Mouthwash may also help.

Heightened sensitivity to sunlight. Use a sunscreen with a minimum SPF (sun protection factor) of 15 while outdoors during the daylight hours. Wearing a hat with a wide brim, a long-sleeved shirt, and long pants is also a good idea.

Weight gain. The only effective remedy is exercise and reduced calorie intake. If weight gain is severe (more than 10 lbs.) and dieting and exercise are not effective, ask your doctor about trying a different drug.

Amoxapine

Insomnia. Take the medication in the morning.*

Monoamine Oxidase Inhibitors

Dizziness, low blood pressure. Rise slowly and carefully from a sitting position or after lying down. Drink plenty of fluids throughout the day. Avoid using saunas or becoming dehydrated.

Hypertensive crisis. See page 31 for foods and drugs that must be avoided or limited to prevent this serious side effect.

Insomnia. Take the medication in the morning.*

Sleepiness. Take the medication 30 minutes before going to bed.*

Swollen fingers and ankles. Swelling usually goes down after the initial period of drug use.

Weight gain. Diet and exercise may help counteract this problem. If weight gain is more than 10 lbs., you may have to discontinue the drug. Most people lose extra weight after the drug is stopped.

Serotonin Reuptake Inhibitors

Dizziness upon standing. Get up slowly after sitting or lying down.

Drowsiness. Take the medication in one dose 30 minutes before bed time.*

Insomnia. Take the medication in the morning.*

*Check with your doctor.

weeks, and each of the tricyclics is believed to be equally effective.

Treatment is started with a small dose and careful monitoring for side effects. The dose is often raised to a therapeutic level over the course of several weeks, but a more gradual increase may lessen the development of side effects, which tend to diminish with continued use. For the elderly, doses are usually 30 to 50% lower than those indicated in the chart on pages 28-29. When the proper dose is established, medications can be taken at bedtime to help induce sleep, rather than causing drowsiness during the day.

Six weeks of treatment are needed before deciding that a tricyclic antidepressant is not working. During this period blood tests may be obtained frequently to ensure that the blood level of the drug is high enough to exert a therapeutic effect—but not so high as to be toxic. Failure to improve may be due to ineffectiveness of the medication or lack of compliance by the patient. About a third of patients stop taking tricyclics because of side effects, and about two-thirds of older patients miss one-quarter to one-half of their doses. Poor compliance leads to fluctuating blood levels and an unfavorable response.

The most prominent side effects of tricyclics are: sedation; dizziness upon standing, due to a drop in blood pressure (orthostatic hypotension); a fine tremor of the hands; nausea and vomiting; blurred vision; dry mouth; rapid heart rate; difficulty urinating; and constipation. In elderly individuals, orthostatic hypotension can lead to falls and broken bones. Many of these side effects can be managed, however. Pilocarpine eye drops may alleviate the blurred vision. Divided doses of bethanechol may be prescribed to counteract problems in urinating. Other techniques to overcome bothersome side effects—such as dry mouth and constipation—are listed in the box on page 25. Amitriptyline and imipramine are more likely than other tricyclics to cause side effects in older patients.

Tricyclics should not be prescribed for people with closed angle glaucoma, and should be used with caution in men with symptoms of benign prostatic hyperplasia (enlarged prostate), who may develop acute urinary retention. Tricyclics can magnify the depressive effects of alcohol and benzodiazepines (drugs used to treat anxiety). The combination of tricyclics with antihistamines or drugs used to treat Parkinson's disease can lead to severe constipation, fecal impaction, or urinary retention, particularly in the elderly.

Tricyclics were considered the treatment of choice for people with coronary heart disease (CHD) associated with an abnormality in heart rhythm, not only because these drugs are effective in treating depression, but also because they had an antiarrhythmic effect. More recent evidence, however, has suggested that tricyclics might cause life-threatening ventricular fibrillation in individuals who have CHD. In a recent re-evaluation of the subject, the researchers who first discovered the antiarrhythmic effects of tricyclics recommend that these drugs not be used in most individuals with severe CHD, based on theoretical considerations. Despite the cardiac risks of tricyclics, however, their benefit in treating depression must be considered, especially since they may be the only antidepressants that are effective in severely depressed older people.

These researchers recommend first trying other antidepressants—selective serotonin reuptake inhibitors, such as fluoxetine (Prozac), or the dopamine reuptake inhibitor bupropion (Wellbutrin)—in mild to moderately depressed older individuals with se-

NEW RECOMMENDATION

Antidepressants and Parkinson's Medication

Tricyclic antidepressants, such as amitriptyline (Elavil, Endep) or proptriptyline (Vivactil), and selective serotonin reuptake inhibitors (SSRIs) like fluoxetine (Prozac), should not be mixed with the antiparkinsonian drug selegiline (Eldepryl), according to the Food and Drug Administration (FDA).

This past February, the FDA ordered a change in selegiline's package insert to reflect this warning. An interaction between these drugs may cause: high fever, tremors, agitation, restlessness, and, in some cases, death. Other symptoms may include fainting, profuse sweating, seizures, behavioral changes, and stiffened muscles.

Depressed patients suffering from Parkinson's disease should make sure their doctor knows if they are taking selegiline. The FDA recommends allowing 14 days to elapse between stopping selegiline and starting on a tricyclic antidepressant or an SSRI. Patients taking SSRIs, which remain in the body longer than tricyclics, should wait at least five weeks after discontinuing SSRI therapy before beginning to take selegiline.

FDA MEDICAL BULLETIN
VOLUME 25, NUMBER 1
February 1995

vere CHD. If there is no response to these drugs, a tricyclic may be tried. Since the risk of ventricular fibrillation from tricyclics increases with the severity of CHD, the doctor must weigh the depth of the depression against the potential cardiac danger.

Tetracyclics. The mode of action, efficacy, and side effects of maprotiline, the only tetracyclic antidepressant currently available, are similar to those of the tricyclics.

Selective serotonin reuptake inhibitors (SSRIs). With fluoxetine (Prozac) leading the way (it ranks second only to the ulcer drug Zantac in overall U.S. sales), this class of medications has fast become a symbol of easy self-improvement. Due to reports in the popular press, many now view these drugs as a simple way to improve flagging productivity in the business world. However, fluoxetine and other SSRIs are powerful antidepressants, which inhibit the reuptake of serotonin, and thereby raise its concentration in the brain. They are as effective as tricyclics (about half of patients taking an SSRI will have a complete remission) and their side effects are generally milder than most other antidepressants, which has earned them favor among some physicians as a first-line treatment for depression. Compared to tricyclics, particular advantages of these drugs are a low risk of fatal overdoses and less danger of serious disturbances of heart rhythm in people with cardiac disease. In particular, SSRIs are effective against mild-to-moderate depression (dysthymia).

Fluoxetine (Prozac) gained much media attention following reports that it engendered suicidal thoughts, actual suicides, and other violent acts in a small number of patients. There is, however, no good evidence that fluoxetine is more closely associated with suicide than any other treatment for depression. In the particular cases cited in these reports, the drug was apparently not effective in the depressed patients who committed suicide (all of whom had a history of suicidal tendencies), but neither did it prompt the suicides.

Side effect of SSRIs include insomnia or drowsiness, nausea, anxiety, and weight loss. A troublesome side effect is sexual dysfunction, which may occur in as many as one-third of patients taking these drugs and affects both men and women. This problem can take the form of diminished sexual desire, changes in the sensations of arousal, and orgasmic and ejaculatory disturbances. Symptoms usually develop within the first week of starting an SSRI, though for some, they start more slowly as blood levels of the medication build up. Lowering the dosage may reduce sexual dysfunc-

Antidepressant Drugs 1996

Depression is thought to be the result of an imbalance of mood-enhancing neurotransmitters, such as norepinephrine and serotonin, in the central nervous system. Antidepressants offset this imbalance. If the first type of medication taken is not effective, an alternative drug choice will usually be prescribed. Generally, antidepressant drugs become fully effective within three to six weeks after starting them, but improvement sometimes takes longer in older people. This chart lists the most commonly prescribed antidepressants and includes generic and brand names (in parentheses).

Drug type/names	Average daily dosage*	How they work	Comments	Estimated cost**
TRICYCLICS				
amitriptyline (Elavil, Endep)	up to 150 mg	Tricyclic drugs inhibit the reabsorption and inactivation of norepinephrine and/or serotonin by neurons. Since these neurotransmitters are not reabsorbed, they are free to move between nerve cells and can continue to exert their effect.	Widely used. May cause dizziness upon standing, drowsiness, weakness, headache, dry mouth, blurred vision, constipation, nausea, difficulty urinating, or increased appetite (which may include a craving for sweets). Causes skin to be more sensitive to sunlight, and may result in itching, redness, or discoloration of the skin. If protriptyline is taken late in the day, it may interfere with sleep.	amitriptyline, generic (25 mg) $5.79; Elavil (25 mg) $37.26; Endep (25 mg) $30.74
amoxapine (Asendin)	150 to 300 mg			amoxapine, generic (50 mg) $84.03; Asendin (50 mg) $121.29
desipramine (Norpramin)	150 to 250 mg			desipramine, generic (25 mg) $24.26; Norpramin (25 mg) $59.46
doxepin (Sinequan)	50 to 300 mg			doxepin, generic (25 mg) $12.86; Sinequan (25 mg) $43.690
imipramine (Tipramine, Tofranil)	150 to 300 mg			imipramine, generic (25 mg) $4.81; Tipramine (25 mg) $3.06; Tofranil (25 mg) $43.63
nortriptyline (Aventyl, Pamelor)	50 to 150 mg			nortriptyline, generic (25 mg) $72.75; Aventyl (25 mg) $83.24; Pamelor (25 mg) $90.96
protriptyline (Vivactil)	15 to 40 mg			Vivactil (5 mg) $45.05
trimipramine (Surmontil)	100 to 250 mg			Surmontil (25 mg) $62.99
TETRACYCLICS				
maprotiline (Ludiomil)	100 to 225 mg	Similar to tricyclics.	Blurred vision, dizziness or lightheadedness (especially in the elderly), drowsiness, weakness, dry mouth, headache, skin rash, impotence, and increased or decreased sexual drive may occur.	maprotiline, generic (25 mg) $32.59; Ludiomil (25 mg) $44.34
MAO INHIBITORS				
phenelzine (Nardil)	15 to 60 mg	Monoamine oxidase (MAO) is an enzyme in the body that inactivates the neurotransmitters that carry chemical messages between neurons. MAO inhibitors block the enzyme MAO and allow more chemical messages between neurons.	May cause dizziness or lightheadedness (especially in older patients), drowsiness, headache, insomnia, decreased sexual function, or weight gain. Foods containing tyramine (see page 31) should be avoided, since they may cause a sudden, severe rise in blood pressure. MAO inhibitors may interact dangerously with numerous other drugs.	Nardil (15 mg) $38.32
tranylcypromine (Parnate)	20 to 30 mg			Parnate (10 mg) $43.60
isocarboxazid				Price not available; isocarboxazid available only upon special request to manufacturer.

Antidepressant Drugs 1996 (continued)

Drug type/names	Average daily dosage*	How they work	Comments	Estimated cost**
SEROTONIN REUPTAKE INHIBITORS				
fluoxetine (Prozac)	10 to 40 mg	These drugs block the reabsorption and inactivation of serotonin by neurons. This increases the availability of serotonin to carry messages between nerve cells.	May cause anxiety, nervousness, insomnia, drowsiness, weakness, headache, diarrhea, increased sweating, nausea, decreased sexual function, or dizziness. Nefazodone may cause fewer cases of insomnia and sexual dysfunction.	Prozac (20 mg) $215.82
nefazodone (Serzone)	50 to 300 mg			Serzone (100 mg) $82.80
paroxetine (Paxil)	20 to 50 mg			Paxil (20 mg) $185.65
sertraline (Zoloft)	50 to 200 mg			Zoloft (50 mg) $194.11
trazodone (Desyrel)	100 to 400 mg			trazodone, generic (50 mg) $26.35; Desyrel (50 mg) $123.18
DOPAMINE REUPTAKE INHIBITORS bupropion (Wellbutrin)	75 to 300 mg	These drugs block the reabsorption and inactivation of dopamine, which is both a neurotransmitter and a precursor of other neurotransmitters.	May cause agitation or restlessness, tremor, severe headache, trouble sleeping, constipation, appetite loss, dry mouth, increased sweating, and nausea or vomiting. Alcohol use increases risk of seizures.	Wellbutrin (100 mg) $75.11
SEROTONIN AND NOREPINEPHRINE REUPTAKE INHIBITORS venlafaxine (Effexor)	75 to 300 mg	These drugs block the reabsorption and inactivation of serotonin and norepinephrine, increasing the availability of these neurotransmitters.	May cause weakness, increased sweating, nausea, drowsiness, dry mouth, dizziness, constipation, nervousness, sexual dysfunction, or appetite loss. May increase blood pressure in some patients; regular blood pressure monitoring is advisable.	Effexor (50 mg) $94.28
ANTIMANICS				
lithium (Eskalith, Lithobid)	Dose is variable, and is determined by measuring blood levels of the drug.	Action not established.	Lithium may cause excessive thirst, frequent urination, hand tremor, weight gain, lethargy, or nausea. Carbamazepine may cause dizziness, unsteadiness, or nausea, especially when first started. With valproate, nausea and other gastrointestinal symptoms, appetite loss, hand tremor, transient hair loss, and weight gain or loss may occur.	lithium carbonate, generic (300 mg) $7.81; Eskalith (300 mg) $16.10; Lithobid (300 mg) $23.69
carbamazepine (Epitol, Tegretol)	400 to 2,000 mg	Action not established.		carbamazepine, generic (200 mg) $23.74; Epitol (200 mg) $24.00; Tegretol (200 mg) $36.05
valproate (Depakene, Depakote Sprinkles)	500 to 1,500 mg	Action not established.		valproic acid, generic (250 mg) $34.08; Depakene (250 mg) $111.98; Depakote Sprinkles (125 mg) $29.95

*These dosages represent an average range for the treatment of depression. The precise effective dosage varies from patient to patient and depends on many factors. Do not make any changes in your medication without consulting your doctor. Starting dosages for older patients tend to be lower.

**Average wholesale prices to pharmacists for 100 tablets or capsules of the dosage amount listed in parentheses. Costs to consumers are higher.

Source: *Red Book, 1995* (Medical Economics Data, publishers).

tion, but it raises the possibility that depressive symptoms will recur. Certain drugs—for example, the dopamine reuptake inhibitor bupropion (Wellbutrin)—can be used in conjunction with an SSRI to alleviate adverse sexual effects, but the additional drugs can create new problems as well. Changing to a different class of drugs that is less likely to cause sexual dysfunction, usually to bupropion, may also help.

A new drug with some SSRI properties, called nefazodone (Serzone), was approved for use by the Food and Drug Administration (FDA) in December 1994. Its manufacturer claims that it has fewer sexual side effects than other SSRIs, but further research will be necessary to verify this. Studies have found doses of nefazodone ranging from 50 to 300 milligrams a day to be as effective as imipramine, which is commonly used as a benchmark to gauge other antidepressants. Nefazodone's side effects are similar to those of other drugs in its class.

Dopamine reuptake inhibitors. Bupropion, another second-generation antidepressant, interferes with the reuptake of dopamine, which is a neurotransmitter itself and a precursor of other neurotransmitters. This drug causes less sedation and fewer other side effects than the tricyclics.

Monoamine oxidase (MAO) inhibitors. Like tricyclics, MAO inhibitors increase brain levels of norepinephrine and serotonin, in this case by blocking the action of the enzyme MAO, which normally inactivates the two neurotransmitters. MAO inhibitors are effective in many depressed patients, especially those whose depression is accompanied by marked anxiety, panic attacks, heightened appetite, or excessive sleeping. The results of one small study suggests that the MAO inhibitor selegiline (Eldepryl), a drug commonly used to treat Parkinson's disease, may be helpful to older adults whose depression has not responded to other drugs or, for some, to electroconvulsive therapy.

These drugs can cause some of the same side effects as the tricyclics. MAO inhibitors should not be used by patients with active alcoholism, congestive heart failure, or severe impairment of liver or kidney function, or by those who are taking multiple medications for hypertension.

Of particular concern is the danger of a sudden extreme elevation in blood pressure (hypertensive crisis) when people taking MAO inhibitors use certain drugs or eat foods containing tyramine (see the box on page 31). Normally, the enzyme MAO destroys the tyramine consumed in the diet and prevents its blood-pressure-rais-

NEW RESEARCH

New Prozac Side Effects Uncovered

A four-year study of over 5,500 patients taking the antidepressant fluoxetine (Prozac) showed that some experienced a rare type of reaction referred to as extrapyramidal side effects. These produce symptoms like those of Parkinson's disease, such as impaired muscle tone, tremors and spasms, or feelings of restlessness, which can reach the point of being unable to sit down. Fortunately, these effects were rare, occurring in only 15 of the subjects (0.27%). By comparison, the most common, but less disabling, fluoxetine side effects—agitation and anxiety—occurred in 31 of patients (0.56%).

Extrapyramidal side effects developed within several days to 10 months after starting on fluoxetine, but disappeared or improved in 12 of the 15 patients once the medication was withdrawn. Higher doses did not appear to increase the risk of these effects. (Most patients took 20 mg a day, while larger doses ranged up to 80 mg daily.) Patients experiencing these types of symptoms should contact their doctor before stopping their medication. The rarity of these side effects means that they will be a very infrequent reason for discontinuation.

AMERICAN JOURNAL OF PSYCHIATRY
VOLUME 152, NUMBER 1
January 1995

Food and Drug Restrictions for MAO Inhibitors

MAO inhibitors are not usually a first-line choice for the treatment of depression because of potentially dangerous food and drug interactions. People taking these drugs must avoid foods high in tyramine, which may cause a dangerous rise in blood pressure (hypertensive crisis). In addition, MAO inhibitors cannot be taken at the same time as a number of over-the-counter and prescription drugs. The following are some of the foods and drugs that interact with MAO inhibitors. If you intend to begin MAO inhibitor therapy, discontinue use of all of the listed foods and drugs. If you must take one of the drugs listed, do not take MAO inhibitors; ask your doctor to prescribe another type of antidepressant.

Foods

- Avocados, very ripe
- Bananas, very ripe
- Beer, ale, liqueurs, sherry, Chianti wine
- Caffeinated beverages*
- Caviar
- Cheese, except cottage, cream, and farmer cheese
- Chocolate*
- Fava beans
- Fish—smoked, salted, pickled, cured, or dried
- Game, aged
- Liver (beef or chicken)
- Meat—smoked, salted, pickled, cured, or dried
- Sausage, dried or fermented
- Sour cream*
- Soy sauce*
- Yeast extracts; brewers' yeast
- Yogurt*

Medications

- Antidepressant medications, including tricyclics and serotonin reuptake inhibitors
- Caffeine-containing medications, such as stimulants and diet pills
- Cold or allergy medicines
- Cough medicine, except guaifenesin
- Epinephrine, ephedrine, norepinephrine, phenylephrine, cocaine, and other similar drugs
- Levodopa (Dopar, Larodopa), used to treat Parkinson's disease
- Local anesthetics containing epinephrine
- Meperidine (Demerol), a prescription pain reliever
- Methyldopa (Aldomet), used to treat hypertension
- Nasal decongestants or asthma inhalers

*May be consumed in small quantities.

ing effects; this protective mechanism cannot take place when the action of MAO in the liver and intestine is blocked by an MAO inhibitor. Symptoms of a hypertensive crisis include severe chest pain, severe headache, sweating and clammy skin, and nausea and vomiting. Immediate treatment of a hypertensive crisis with blood-pressure-lowering drugs is essential. The dietary restrictions imposed by MAO inhibitors have relegated them to second-choice drugs for the treatment of depression.

Lithium and other antimanics. Although its mechanism of action remains unknown, lithium is the first-choice drug for treating acute manic episodes and preventing recurrences of mania and depression in those with bipolar illness. Overall, about 50 to 80% of patients will have some response to lithium. It is generally safe when used correctly. Lithium is contraindicated in patients with seriously impaired kidney function, and lower doses are prescribed in elderly individuals. Blood levels of lithium are measured regularly to assure adequate doses and to avoid the dangerous effects of toxic levels.

Common adverse effects of lithium include increased thirst and urination, nausea and vomiting, loss of appetite, diarrhea, a fine tremor of the hand, and muscle weakness. Among the manifestations of toxicity are muscle twitching, coarse tremor, slurred speech, drowsiness, disorientation, confusion, seizures, and coma. Diuretics, such as furosemide (Lasix) or hydrochlorothiazide (Esidrix), and nonsteroidal anti-inflammatory drugs, such as ibuprofen (Advil, Motrin), increase the risk of toxicity. Long-term treatment with lithium can compromise kidney function. About one-quarter of those taking the drug develop persistent thirst and excessive urination due to its effect on the kidneys. Also, by decreasing the secretion of thyroid hormone, lithium can produce hypothyroidism. These effects are usually completely reversed once lithium is discontinued.

Two other drugs, valproate (Depakene, Depakote) and carbamazepine (Epitol, Tegretol), are used for treating bipolar illness. Along with lithium, they are referred to as mood-stabilizing medications. Although less research is available on these drugs than on lithium, one recent study found that 48% of patients with acute mania taking valproate had at least a 50% reduction in manic symptoms—a rate similar to that for lithium. Carbamazepine also appears to be effective, but presently, there are no data comparing it to lithium. Lithium is the only one of these drugs proven to be effective during maintenance treatment.

Most of valproate's and carbamazepine's side effects can be relieved by dose adjustment. However, valproate can also cause dangerous effects on the bone marrow, liver, and pancreas, which have to be monitored by blood tests. Carbamazepine can cause blood dyscrasias (abnormalities), hepatic failure, dermatitis, and pancreatitis. Although these side effects are rare, laboratory tests cannot reliably screen for them. Patients should be aware of the signs of trouble for both drugs—easy bruising and yellow jaundice.

Additional drugs. Since two to three weeks may pass before mood-stabilizing drugs take effect, many patients may need additional medication to control psychotic symptoms. Benzodiazepines, such as alprazolam (Xanax) or lorazepam (Ativan), or neuroleptics, such as haloperidol (Haldol), are both used for this purpose.

NEW RESEARCH

Treating Relapse of Depression

A recent study tested the belief that patients who are successfully treated with one type of antidepressant during their initial bout with depression will respond to that drug again in the event of a relapse. The study involved 12 patients, age 20 to 66, with either pure dysthymia or dysthymia with major depression. All participants had achieved full or partial remission after 26 weeks on the tricyclic antidepressant desipramine (Norpramin), but relapsed after drug therapy was discontinued. Researchers began treating them again with desipramine at the same or higher dosages.

After an average of 4.7 weeks, 11 of the 12 patients (91.7%) reached full remission—a "remarkably high proportion," according to the study authors. They also pointed out that some patients needed seven to eight weeks before responding—indicating the possible benefits of extending the initial trial of a drug beyond the standard six weeks. Further study will be necessary to reaffirm these findings because of the small number of patients involved and the lack of a comparison group of subjects taking a placebo, but the results clearly support the common practice of using a previously successful drug to retreat chronically depressed patients suffering from relapse.

AMERICAN JOURNAL OF PSYCHIATRY
VOLUME 152, NUMBER 6
June 1995

Comparing Side Effects in Common Antidepressant Drugs

All classes of drugs used to treat depression have the potential to cause side effects. The severity of these adverse symptoms varies from patient to patient and depends on many factors, including age, genetics, and overall health. For example, the same drug and dosage may cause mild and transient drowsiness in a younger patient, but an older patient may experience sedation so bothersome that the drug must be discontinued. Many side effects are most severe during the initiation of drug treatment or just after a dosage increase, and tend to diminish over time. Nonetheless, the likelihood of both short- and long-term side effects is one of the key considerations that a doctor weighs when choosing which drug to prescribe for a particular patient. This chart gives a general overview of the relative severity of certain side effects for most of the major antidepressants.

Drugs	Anti-cholinergic symptoms†	Drowsiness	Insomnia, agitation	Orthostatic hypotension††	Cardiac arrhythmia	Gastro-intestinal problems	Weight gain (more than 13 lbs.)
Amitriptyline	•••••	•••••	•	•••••	••••	•	•••••
Amoxapine	•••	•••	•••	•••	••••	•	••
Bupropion	•	•	•••	•	••	••	•
Desipramine	••	••	••	•••	•••	•	••
Doxepin	••••	•••••	•	•••	•••	•	••••
Fluoxetine	•	•	•••	•	•	••••	•
Imipramine	••••	••••	••	•••••	••••	••	••••
MAO inhibitors§	••	••	•••	•••	•	••	•••
Maprotiline	•••	•••••	•	•	••	•	•••
Nortriptyline	••	••	•	•••	•••	•	••
Paroxetine	•	•	•••	•	•	••••	•
Protriptyline	•••	••	••	•••	•••	•	•
Sertraline	•	•	•••	•	•	••••	•
Trazodone	•	•••••	•	••	••	••	••
Trimipramine	••	•••••	•	•••	•••	•	••••

• = Rare or none •• to ••• = Moderately common •••• to ••••• = Relatively common

†Dry mouth, blurred vision, urinary hesitancy, or constipation.
††Dizziness upon standing up after sitting or lying down, due to a sudden drop in blood pressure.
§Monoamine oxidase inhibitors (isocarboxazid, phenelzine, tranylcypromine).

Source: U.S. Department of Health and Human Services, Agency for Health Care Policy and Research, *Depression in Primary Care: Volume 2. Treatment of Major Depression,* Clinical Practice Guideline No. 5, April 1993.

Benzodiazepines are usually safer, but neuroleptics are needed when symptoms are severe.

Electroconvulsive Therapy (ECT)

Electroconvulsive therapy has an important place in the treatment of depression and, less commonly, hard-to-treat mania. ECT has a high success rate for depression, and improvement occurs more rapidly than with any other form of treatment. Previously, the procedure was reserved for those with depression so severe that it was life-threatening, or those who failed to respond to psychotherapy and medications. In recent years, however, its use has widened to

Depression and Anxiety in Late Life

Depression and anxiety disorders constitute a major health problem among the elderly; yet they often remain undiagnosed and untreated. Older adults tend to be embarrassed and reluctant to seek professional help for emotional problems, partly because the stigma of psychiatric illness is especially strong among people in this age group. In addition, friends and family often fail to perceive signs of distress.

Primary care physicians also may not recognize these disorders, largely because anxious or depressed older patients are more likely to describe physical complaints, rather than subjective feelings of anxiety or a depressed mood. For example, depressed patients may report loss of appetite, insomnia, lack of energy, or loss of interest and enjoyment in daily activities; patients suffering from anxiety might complain of vague gastrointestinal distress, heart palpitations, or sleep disturbances. Unfortunately, these symptoms are often seen by both doctor and patient as a "normal part of aging" that accompanies the physical, social, and economic problems commonly faced by older adults.

Once depression or anxiety is suspected, the precise cause of the disorder is more difficult to determine in older patients. The elderly are typically subjected to numerous stressful life conditions: loss of a spouse, family, or friends by death or geographic relocation; retirement, which may be accompanied by a loss of status and self-identity; diminished financial resources; fears of death or loss of independence and self-sufficiency; social isolation; and medical problems. Any of these factors may trigger symptoms of depression or anxiety.

In addition, the higher prevalence of concurrent medical conditions and medications in older people further complicates the diagnosis. Depression in late life may be a primary disorder, but may also result from some underlying organic cause, such as cancer, stroke, or a reaction to a prescription drug. Anxiety is often caused by an underlying disorder, for example, hyperthyroidism, irregular heart rhythm, chronic lung disease, or nutritional deficiency, or by a prescription or over-the-counter drug.

The possibility of dementia adds further difficulties. The symptoms of major depression can mimic those of a dementing disease, such as Alzheimer's (e.g., disorientation, distractibility, memory loss). On the other hand, a patient in the first stages of dementia may experience anxiety due to perceived memory changes and cognitive decline. Thus, doctors need to perform a careful mental status examination, as well as a medical history and physical exam, to determine the primary cause of the psychological symptoms.

A correct diagnosis itself may help to alleviate symptoms; for example, mild anxiety can often be relieved merely by recognizing the problem and providing simple reassurance, reducing social isolation, or teaching relaxation techniques. Oftentimes, however, more active and vigorous intervention is necessary, including group or individual psychotherapy or treatment with antidepressant or antianxiety drugs.

In mild cases, it is usually better to try more conservative treatments first. Drug therapy must be approached with caution, because older patients are more susceptible to adverse side effects than younger ones. They generally require smaller dosages, as well as closer monitoring for a toxic reaction and to see that drugs are taken regularly. Moreover, many older people have concurrent medical conditions or medical prescriptions that may interfere with the action of antidepressant or antianxiety drugs. Treatment can also be difficult in reluctant patients or those lacking a social support system to help them orchestrate practical considerations, such as transportation and cost.

Despite all of these obstacles, however, treatment for both depression and anxiety in older patients is generally very effective; even partial success can lead to improved quality of life and productivity. As the number of elderly in the U.S. continues to grow, the need for a better understanding of the diagnosis and treatment of these disorders in late life is becoming increasingly important.

include depression associated with delusions. In part, use of ECT has been limited by its undeserved poor reputation among the lay public, who have the impression that ECT is dangerous and leads to brain damage. The nature of the ECT technique undoubtedly contributes to these concerns: a controlled seizure lasting about 40 seconds is produced by attaching electrodes to the head and sending a small amount of electrical current through the brain for one to two seconds. Many people have been frightened by witnessing a spontaneous seizure, and the notion of passing electricity through the brain conjures up horror-movie images. But, in addition to its relatively rapid and frequent benefits, ECT is safer than either tricyclic drugs or lithium. Since its introduction in the 1940s, the safety of ECT has been improved by refinements in the delivery of the electrical stimulus, the administration of muscle-relaxing drugs to prevent physical injury during the seizure, and the use of general anesthesia to eliminate discomfort.

Elevated intracranial pressure is the only absolute medical contraindication to ECT. Caution is necessary in people who have suffered a recent heart attack or who have a history of abnormal heart rhythm, but a recent study found that ECT can be used safely in individuals with severe cardiac disease, provided that the patients are closely monitored for any sign of cardiac abnormality during and immediately following the procedure. Researchers performed ECT on 40 depressed patients with cardiac disease and on 40 depressed patients without cardiac disease, taking special note of the types of cardiac disturbances that occurred in both groups. Fifty-five percent of those in the cardiac group experienced heart abnormalities as a result of ECT, but most of the episodes were transitory—that is, they occurred during or right after ECT and resolved immediately. In the non-cardiac group, 7.5% had cardiac complications during ECT; all were transitory. The type of prior cardiac disease strongly predicted the type of cardiac abnormality, if any, that occurred during ECT. For example, a history of arrhythmias was predictive of arrhythmias during ECT. Five patients developed ischemic events, including one heart attack; all had a previous history of ischemic heart disease or heart attacks. This information allows doctors to use appropriate preventive measures to reduce the risk of cardiac complications during ECT.

One major side effect of ECT is transient confusion right after each treatment; other immediate side effects are nausea, headaches, or muscle soreness. Some patients experience some memory loss, but it usually lasts for no longer than a month.

ECT is considered the preferred treatment in those who have not responded to medications, have a medical illness that precludes antidepressant use, or whose depression is particularly severe, especially if they have had success with ECT in the past. The greatest use of ECT is in individuals older than 61, even though post-ECT confusion increases with advancing age. Approximately half of medication-resistant patients respond after a course of 6 to 12 ECT treatments. Relapse is common unless ECT is followed by antidepressant medication or lithium.

Anxiety Disorders

Anxiety is a common, normal, and at times useful response that may improve performance when facing life's challenges and dangers. But in some people, anxiety spins out of control. Anxiety disorders are characterized by either recurrent or persistent psychological and physical symptoms that interfere with normal function; symptoms continue in the absence of obvious external stresses, or they are excessive responses to these stresses. Anxiety does not result from an abnormal perception of risk. In research comparing how healthy people and those with an anxiety disorder assess the risk of 22 different events (all but two of which were negative) happening to themselves or to another person, the estimations were almost identical. Both groups overestimated the risk of rare events and underestimated the risk of common events, and both underestimated the risk of events happening to themselves, as opposed to others.

Common psychological symptoms of anxiety include irritability, a "keyed-up" feeling, intense fear, worry, and difficulty concentrating. These are accompanied by physical manifestations such as sweating, dry mouth, hot flashes or chills, dizziness, palpitations, muscle tension, trembling, and restlessness. Some medical conditions and drugs can either cause anxiety or produce its symptoms. Examples of such conditions are alcohol withdrawal, asthma, heart attack, hyperthyroidism, and even a deficiency in folate or vitamin B_{12}. Drugs that might cause or mimic anxiety symptoms include bronchodilators, such as ephedrine (Ephed II) or epinephrine (Primatene Mist and others); psychostimulants, such as methylphenidate (Ritalin); phenylpropanolamine (Acutrim and others); and thyroid hormone.

Some evidence suggests that chronic anxiety may lead to long-term health problems, such as hypertension. An 18- to 20-year follow-up of individuals who participated in the Framingham Heart Study found such a connection in middle-aged men. None of the men had hypertension at the start of the study. To evaluate psychological traits that may be relevant to hypertension, participants were asked about levels of anxiety, feelings of anger, and expression of anger. Men who were 45 to 59 years old and had a high score for anxiety at the start of the study were twice as likely to develop hypertension as men who did not have anxiety symptoms. Moreover, heart attack risk may also be increased by anxiety. A study of 30,000 men, ages 42 to 77, found that those who scored highest on a ques-

NEW RESEARCH

The Social Costs of Anxiety

In order to measure some of the social consequences of anxiety disorders, data from interviews with over 18,500 U.S. men and women were reviewed in a new study. Over 6% of the men and 13% of the women had suffered from an anxiety disorder within the six months preceding the interview. Phobias were the most common type of anxiety disorder, affecting 5.7% of men and 12% of women. The prevalence of panic disorder was 0.5% in men and 1% in women; some 20% of the men and 30% of the women with this disorder also suffered from major depression.

The social impact of anxiety included increased use of medical care, unemployment, and need for disability payments. For example, almost 30% of those with panic disorder sought medical care for emotional, alcohol, or drug-related problems in the six months before the interview, compared to 10% of those without an anxiety disorder. About 25% of men with panic disorder and 18% of obsessive-compulsive men were unemployed for the last five years, compared to 5% of men without such disorders. Men with panic disorder were also about six times more likely to receive disability payments.

This study makes it clear that anxiety disorders not only cause individual impairment, but have a larger social effect as well.

BRITISH JOURNAL OF PSYCHIATRY
VOLUME 166, SUPPLEMENT 27
April 1995

Prevalence of Affective and Anxiety Disorders in the U.S.

Psychiatric disorders may be more common than previously believed, according to results from the recent National Comorbidity Study (NCS). Overall, the NCS estimates—which were compiled by administering a psychiatric interview to a national sample of more than 8,000 people, age 15 to 54—were higher than in previous population studies. Nearly half of the study subjects had experienced at least one disorder during their lifetime, though the majority of all the disorders occurred in a small percentage of high-risk patients. The graph below shows the percent of people who ever experienced an affective or an anxiety disorder during their lifetime, according to NCS data. These rates may be higher compared to other estimates due in part to differences in the way that the NCS was conducted; but in any case, they clearly add further evidence that depression and anxiety pose a major health problem in the U.S.

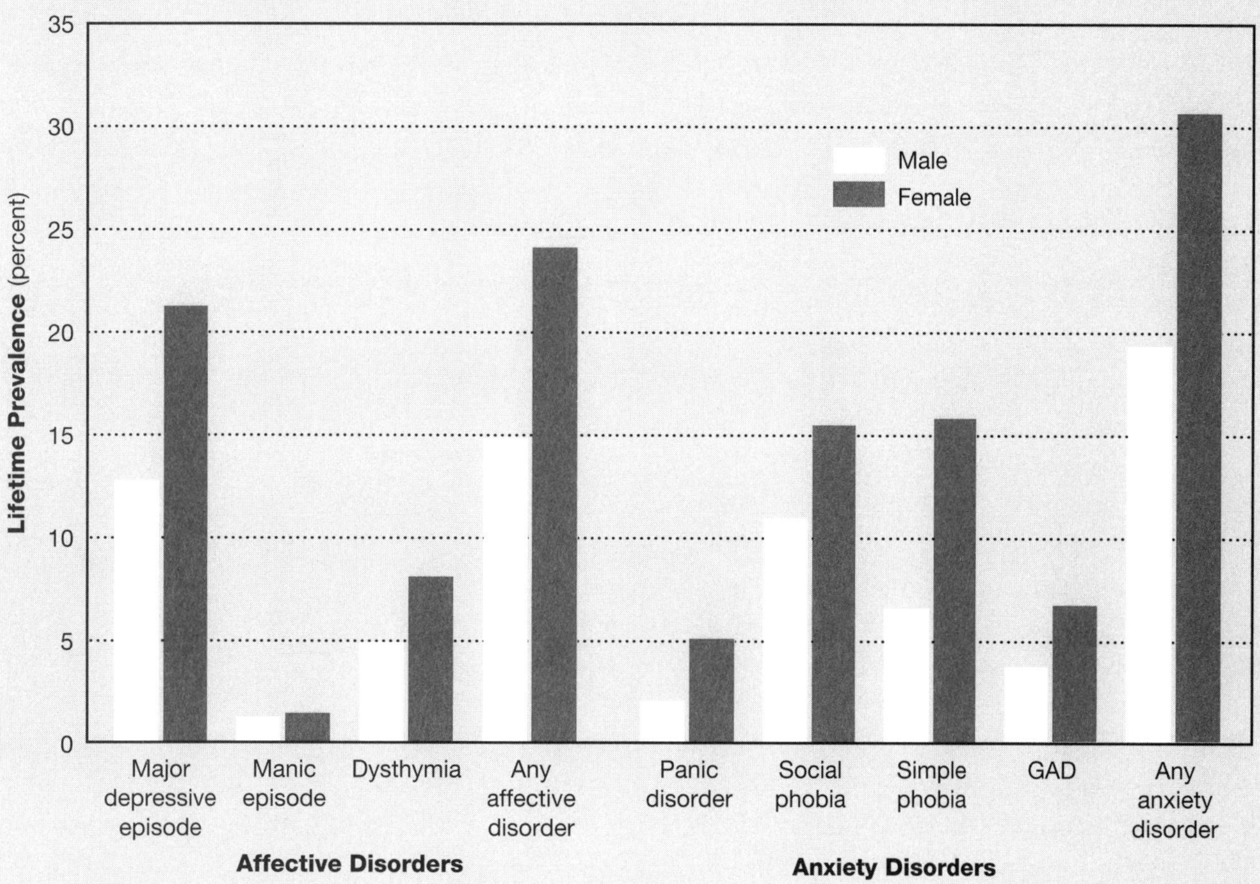

Source: *Archives of General Psychiatry,* January 1994.

tionnaire measuring common phobias had a three-times greater risk of a subsequent fatal heart attack than the men with the lowest scores. The researchers also found that this result was not due to the use of antianxiety drugs. It is possible that the fatal heart attacks may have resulted from some physical consequence of phobic anxiety, such as a type of heart arrhythmia or hyperventilation leading to spasm of a coronary artery.

Anxiety disorders have been broken down into anxiety states

CASE STUDY: PANIC DISORDER

A 62-year-old high school science teacher was evaluated by a physician for complaints of intermittent dizziness and lightheadedness, which had been occurring for about one year. These "attacks" usually lasted two or three seconds and were accompanied by an uncomfortable feeling. After extensive cardiac and neurologic testing, no physical explanation could be found. An evaluation by a psychiatrist revealed that these episodes often came on after upsetting interactions with students, and were accompanied by a feeling of extreme fear. There were no associated feelings of rapid heart beat or shortness of breath. A diagnosis of panic disorder was made and medication begun. The episodes have fully subsided, even though the most common precipitant of the attacks—disturbing incidents with students—has not stopped.

(panic disorder, generalized anxiety disorder, obsessive-compulsive disorder, and post-traumatic stress disorder) and phobic disorders.

Panic Disorder

The cardinal features of panic disorder are short-lived, sudden, unexpected attacks of terror and fear of losing control; attacks begin without warning during nonthreatening activities. Affected individuals often go to an emergency room or consult a cardiologist because their physical symptoms—severe difficulty in breathing, a pounding, rapid heart rate, and a choking sensation—make them believe they are dying or having a heart attack (patients with any question about whether or not they are having a heart attack should see a doctor immediately). An attack generally peaks within 10 minutes and dissipates within 20 to 30 minutes. Panic attacks are characterized by some combination of the following symptoms:

- shortness of breath or hyperventilation
- heart palpitations or a racing pulse
- discomfort in the chest
- dizziness or feeling faint
- choking, nausea, or stomach pain
- sweating
- hot or cold flashes
- trembling or shaking
- sense of unreality; feeling detached from surroundings
- tingling or numbness
- fear of dying or losing one's mind.

Panic disorder is closely related to the mood disorders: Both may occur in the same patient and in members of families with affective disorders, and both may respond to antidepressant medications.

The prevalence of panic disorder is 1 to 2% in both men and women. Attacks commonly begin in the late teens or early twenties and are often neither diagnosed nor treated properly. One estimate suggests that only one in four people with panic attacks receives appropriate care.

The most common complication of panic disorder is agoraphobia—fear of being in public places, especially when alone—which develops as a result of trying to avoid situations that have triggered panic attacks in the past. Left untreated, panic attacks and agoraphobia can markedly restrict an individual's lifestyle, since he or she will attempt to avoid circumstances that might provoke another attack. Although anxiety disorders are more of a problem for younger adults, most cases of agoraphobia are of recent onset in older adults, according to a review of studies. Panic disorder is also complicated by an increased frequency of major depression, alcohol and drug dependency, and suicide.

Generalized Anxiety Disorder (GAD)

Generalized anxiety disorder (GAD) is characterized by a nearly constant state of excessive anxiety and worry without the sudden fluctuations observed in panic disorder. In most cases, the anxiety is unrealistic and irrational, but it can seriously affect thinking and behavior. This disorder occurs in an estimated 2 to 3% of the population and is twice as common in women as in men. Even though GAD is associated with less social and occupational impairment than the other anxiety disorders, the discomfort of chronic anxiety can interfere with a person's ability to enjoy life. To be diagnosed with GAD, six of the following symptoms must be present in a patient for at least six months:

- feeling on edge
- easily startled
- difficulty concentrating
- irritability
- impatience
- insomnia
- trembling
- restlessness, an inability to relax
- muscle tension or aches
- excessive fatigue
- shortness of breath
- accelerated heart rate
- light-headedness, dizziness

NEW FINDINGS

Panic Disorder, Anxiety, and Depression

Recent results suggest that both anxiety and depression symptoms occur frequently in patients with panic disorder. Researchers evaluated 62 women and men previously diagnosed with panic disorder for symptoms of depression and general anxiety. Overall, 61% of the subjects reported two or more significant symptoms of depression. Fatigue, sleep disturbance, loss of interest, difficulty concentrating, and feelings of guilt or worthlessness were the most common. Changes in appetite or weight and thoughts of death were uncommon. Similarly, about three quarters of patients had six or more significant symptoms of generalized anxiety disorder, especially: feelings of tension, easy fatigue, restlessness, irritability, and difficulty concentrating (a symptom of both anxiety and depression).

It is possible that the symptoms of panic disorder can overshadow those caused by another mental illness that requires separate treatment (although in some cases, anxiety symptoms may be due to the panic disorder itself). Even if separate treatment is not necessary, a hidden second illness can still impact on how the primary illness should be handled. Thus, further research is needed to clarify the relationship between these diseases.

THE JOURNAL OF NERVOUS AND MENTAL DISEASE
VOLUME 183, NUMBER 5
May 1995

- dry mouth
- nausea, diarrhea
- excessive sweating
- hot or cold spells
- frequent urination
- trouble swallowing, lump in throat.

Obsessive-Compulsive Disorder (OCD)

Obsessive-compulsive disorder (OCD) is marked by recurrent, repetitive thoughts (obsessions) and/or behaviors (compulsions). (However, an individual with this disorder doesn't necessarily have both obsessions and compulsions.) The person recognizes that the obsessions or compulsive behaviors are unreasonable, but cannot resist thinking or doing them. The obsessions or compulsions often interfere with the sufferer's day-to-day activities and relationships with others.

The symptoms of obsessions and compulsions are as follows:

Obsessions are recurring and persistent thoughts, ideas, images, or impulses, sometimes of an aggressive or violent nature, that seem to invade a person's consciousness. The sufferer will try to suppress or ignore these uncomfortable thoughts and often recognizes that they are unrealistic. Typical obsessions are fear of contamination from germs and thoughts of violent behavior—such as killing a family member.

Compulsions are ritualistic, repetitive, and purposeful behaviors that are performed according to certain rules or stereotypical patterns. The behavior, while clearly excessive, serves to relieve tension and discomfort. Common compulsions are rechecking to be sure doors are locked, windows are closed, and the iron is unplugged; counting stairs while walking; excessive neatness; rearranging and straightening the contents of a desk; and repetitive hand-washing that accompanies an obsession with dirt and germs.

OCD occurs in 2 to 3% of the population. It most often starts in adolescence or the early 20s. Embarrassed and upset by their behavior, most sufferers try to keep it secret; they usually can function with only minimal interference with daily activities. But obsessive thoughts or compulsive behaviors may be frequent or distressing enough to become incapacitating. The most common complication is probably depression; others include alcoholism, abuse of sleeping pills and tranquilizers, and marked interference with normal social and occupational effectiveness. While some people with OCD experience complete remission, in most, the illness pursues an

NEW RESEARCH

An Antidepressant for Obsessive-Compulsive Disorder

Sertraline (Zoloft), a selective serotonin reuptake inhibitor normally used to treat depression, has recently been shown to aid in controlling the symptoms of obsessive-compulsive disorder (OCD). In a 12-week study, researchers gave 324 patients with OCD either a placebo or 50, 100, or 200 mg of sertraline per day.

Compared with those who were given a placebo, the patients taking sertraline showed significantly greater improvement on each of three measures of treatment efficacy. For example, on one scale, 39% of the sertraline patients were rated as "much improved" or "very much improved," compared to 30% of the placebo patients. The higher doses were no more effective than the lowest dose.

The majority of patients in both the sertraline and placebo groups experienced some mild to moderate adverse reactions. The most significant side effects among sertraline takers were diarrhea, decreased libido, and loss of appetite; these reactions grew more frequent as the dosage rose.

Since the smallest dose was as effective as the largest, and produced fewer side effects, the study's authors recommend starting patients on 50 mg of sertraline per day for at least four weeks before increasing the dose.

ARCHIVES OF GENERAL PSYCHIATRY
VOLUME 52, NUMBER 4
April 1995

episodic course with periods of partial remission. In about 10% of those affected, the course of the obsessive-compulsive disorder is chronic and unchanged.

Post-traumatic Stress Disorder

Post-traumatic stress disorder is a form of acute or chronic psychological stress that follows exposure to a traumatic event such as an earthquake, violent crime (rape, child abuse), torture, accident, or warfare. The symptoms are:

- recurrent, intrusive, and distressing dreams and memories of the trauma
- sudden sense that the event is recurring; flashback perception
- extreme distress when confronted with events that symbolize or resemble the trauma
- attempting to avoid thoughts, feelings, and activities associated with the event
- inability to remember aspects of the trauma
- markedly diminished interest in important activities
- feelings of detachment and estrangement from loved ones
- low expectations for the future
- insomnia
- extreme irritability
- inability to concentrate
- hypervigilance
- exaggerated startle response
- excessive fatigue.

The symptoms of the disorder last at least one month. In the acute syndrome, symptoms begin within six months of the trauma. The chronic syndrome may be delayed in onset until more than six months after the event, or may persist for more than six months afterwards. Following a major natural disaster, it has been estimated that as many as 15% of the civilian population will experience enough distress to require treatment. Complications include anxiety, alcoholism, drug abuse, depression, and marital and occupational problems.

Phobic Disorders

The hallmarks of phobic disorders are persistent irrational fears and avoidance of the specific things (animals, heights, closed spaces), social situations, or activities that induce these fears. One example of a social phobia is an extreme fear that public speaking or participation in other public performances may lead to humilia-

NEW RESEARCH

Social Phobia and Other Anxiety Disorders

An estimated 50% of patients with social phobia also have another form of anxiety, such as generalized anxiety or panic disorder, according to a recent review of studies. In addition, 15% of social phobics also have a history of substance abuse, and 20% have a history of depression. The social phobia seems to precede these other conditions, and often has a genetic basis (relatives of people with social phobia have a three-fold increase in risk for the disorder).

Disentangling social phobias from other conditions should result in better treatment since each may require different therapeutic measures. To start, patients diagnosed with social phobia should be carefully screened for other forms of anxiety, and for major depression and substance abuse. Often, alcohol may serve as "self-medication" for social phobics, and this possibility should be explored in alcohol abusers. Conversely, early identification and treatment of social phobics may avert alcohol dependence. Medications effective at treating both social phobia and depression, such as MAO inhibitors such as phenelzine (Nardil), should be considered in those afflicted with both conditions—while anxiety-relieving drugs that may cause depression as a side effect, such as diazepam (Valium) and lorazepam (Ativan), should be carefully monitored or avoided.

EUROPEAN ARCHIVES OF PSYCHIATRY AND CLINICAL NEUROSCIENCE
VOLUME 244, NUMBER 6
February 1995

CASE STUDY: PHOBIA

A 72-year-old woman was mugged on the sidewalk outside her apartment building. She was not harmed. Over the next several weeks, she became increasingly fearful about leaving her apartment until she was so frightened and worried that she stopped going out altogether. When asked about her concerns, she stated that although being robbed was upsetting, she knew the likelihood of another episode was low, and felt she was "over-reacting." Nonetheless, she felt that "the same thing could happen anywhere, anytime." She missed attending the senior center and seeing her close friends, but each time she began to think about going out, she became more and more tense and afraid—to the point where she felt "paralyzed" by her fear and could not leave. Treatment with a combination of relaxation therapy and discussion about her concerns—coupled with a step-by-step program in which she was first accompanied out of her apartment by a friend for a short while, then for increasing lengths of time, and eventually she began going on her own—led to a complete recovery.

tion. Since some degree of such fear is common, the diagnosis of a phobic disorder is made only when the phobia significantly impairs the individual's social or occupational performance.

TREATMENT OF ANXIETY

Treatment of anxiety does not always require medication. The use of antianxiety drugs depends in part on whether the patient can tolerate his or her symptoms until learning to manage them, whether through education on the causes of anxiety, psychotherapy such as behavioral therapy, or techniques that can include progressive muscle relaxation, biofeedback, and more rarely, yoga, self-hypnosis, and transcendental meditation. In general, these approaches are designed to give people with anxiety a feeling of control over their symptoms. Patients can also help themselves by getting enough sleep, avoiding caffeine and alcohol, and getting moderate exercise (which will aid sleep and improve self-esteem). Depending on the severity of anxiety symptoms, treatment can take place in a primary care physician's office or with a specialized therapist.

General Drug Treatment

Panic disorder more frequently requires long-term drug therapy than other anxiety disorders, such as generalized anxiety disorder, which are often improved by patient education and relaxation measures. Although benzodiazepines (anxiolytics) are still commonly used to treat anxiety, two classes of antidepressant drugs, tricyclics and serotonin reuptake inhibitors, or SSRIs (see pages 24 and 27), have become the first line of treatment for anxiety in many instances. They are not habit-forming and can be effective in low doses. Obviously, antidepressants are clearly indicated when an individual with anxiety is depressed as well. Tricyclics and SSRIs take about two to three weeks to act, making them slower than benzodiazepines, but they do bring an early benefit to anxiety patients in promoting better sleep, which quickly improves daily functioning.

It is thought that benzodiazepines relieve anxiety by enhancing the effects of an inhibitory neurotransmitter, gamma-amino butyric acid (GABA); however, their mechanisms of action are not completely understood. The side effects of benzodiazepines are generally mild. They include: sedation, clumsiness, mild disturbances of thinking, and, in rare instances, depressed ventilation. The most troublesome features of the benzodiazepines are the development of tolerance (decreased effectiveness of a given dose with continued use) and both physical and psychological dependence, especially with long-term use at high doses. Tolerance may cause a person to request, and at times receive, larger and larger doses to maintain benefits. In the case of a relapse, a patient may be switched to an SSRI or a tricyclic drug.

Physical dependence is defined by the development of a specific set of physical symptoms upon withdrawal of a drug. Psychological dependence alludes to a continued desire for the drug after it has been discontinued. Physical and psychological dependence can lead to serious manifestations upon withdrawal of benzodiazepines (including irritability, agitation, restlessness, insomnia, loss of appetite, tremor, muscle aches, and, in some patients, confusion or seizures). The danger of a severe withdrawal can be diminished by using the smallest effective dose of a benzodiazepine for the shortest possible time, and by slowly tapering the drug dose as it is being discontinued.

A newer drug, buspirone (a nonbenzodiazepine) has fewer adverse side effects than other medications used to treat anxiety, but it may be less effective (in particular for panic disorder). Common side effects are dizziness, headache, nervousness, and nausea. However, buspirone does not cause sedation, and abuse is unlikely, since it does not cause tolerance or dependence.

Treatment of Specific Anxiety Disorders

Psychotherapy, medication, and coping behaviors are used to treat all the anxiety disorders. However, research has found that the vari-

Antianxiety Drugs 1996

All of the drugs listed in the chart below, except the last three, are benzodiazepines. Benzodiazepines slow the central nervous system and are primarily used to treat nervousness, tension, and, sometimes, insomnia. They produce a calming effect by depressing activity in the parts of the brain that control emotion. They do this by enhancing the action of the neurotransmitter gamma-amino butyric acid (GABA), which in turn blocks the arousal of higher brain centers. This reduces communication between brain cells. All of the benzodiazepines and meprobamate may be habit forming. MAO inhibitors, tricyclics, and SSRIs (antidepressant drugs covered on pages 28-29) may also be used to treat anxiety.

Generic name	Brand name	Average daily dosage*	Comments	Estimated cost**
alprazolam***	Xanax	0.5 to 4 mg	The most common side effect is drowsiness. This drug may be more habit forming than other benzodiazepines. It has an antidepressant action. It is often prescribed for panic attacks.	alprazolam, generic (0.25 mg) $51.87; Xanax (0.25 mg) $65.89
chlordiazepoxide	Libritabs, Librium	20 to 80 mg	Drowsiness, confusion, and oversedation are all possible side effects.	chlordiazepoxide, generic (5 mg) $5.64, (10 mg) $5.85; Libritabs (5 mg) $33.38; Librium (5 mg) $34.73, (10 mg) $50.56
clonazepam	Klonopin	0.5 to 4 mg	The most common side effect is drowsiness. Decreased muscle coordination is also possible.	Klonopin (0.5 mg) $69.84, (1 mg) $79.66, (2 mg) $113.72
clorazepate	Gen-XENE, Tranxene-SD, Tranxene T-Tab	15 to 60 mg	Drowsiness, dizziness, and nervousness are all possible side effects. Blurred vision, confusion, and depression occur occasionally.	clorazepate, generic (3.75 mg) $24.84, (7.5 mg) $30.25, (15 mg) $45.81; Gen-XENE (3.75 mg) $22.16, (7.5 mg) $27.10, (15 mg) $39.00; Tranxene-SD (11.25 mg) $295.74; Tranxene T-Tab (3.75 mg) $111.76, (7.5 mg) $139.03, (15 mg) $188.64
diazepam	Valium	5 to 15 mg	Drowsiness, lethargy, and a “hangover” effect are all possible side effects.	diazepam, generic (2 mg) $6.29, (5 mg) $9.54; Valium (2 mg) $39.17, (5 mg) $60.93
estazolam***	ProSom	1 to 2 mg at bedtime	Estazolam is often prescribed for insomnia. Drowsiness, dizziness, and abnormal coordination are all possible side effects.	ProSom (1 mg) $85.21, (2 mg) $94.93
flurazepam	Dalmane	15 to 30 mg	Flurazepam is often prescribed for insomnia. Drowsiness, dizziness, fatigue, and lightheadedness are all possible side effects.	flurazepam, generic (15 mg) $20.49, (30 mg) $22.70; Dalmane (15 mg) $53.72, (30 mg) $58.43

Antianxiety Drugs 1996 (continued)

Generic name	Brand name	Average daily dosage*	Comments	Estimated cost**
halazepam	Paxipam	80 to 160 mg	The most common side effect is drowsiness. Dizziness, headache, and disorientation are also possible side effects.	Paxipam (20 mg) $44.74, (40 mg) $62.18
lorazepam***	Ativan	1 to 4 mg	Sedation, dizziness, weakness, and decreased muscle coordination are all possible side effects.	lorazepam, generic (2 mg) $24.91; Ativan (2 mg) $114.78
oxazepam***	Serax	30 to 120 mg	The most common side effect is drowsiness. Dizziness, nausea, vertigo, and headache are also possible side effects.	oxazepam, generic (15 mg) $30.75; Serax (15 mg) $84.45
prazepam	none available	20 to 60 mg	Drowsiness, dizziness, weakness, fatigue, and lightheadedness are all possible side effects.	prazepam, generic (25 gm powder) $24.50
quazepam	Doral	7.5 to 15 mg	The most common side effect is drowsiness. A "hangover" effect is also possible.	Doral (7.5 mg) $87.06, (15 mg) $95.14
temazepam***	Restoril	15 to 30 mg	Drowsiness, dizziness, lethargy, and confusion are all possible side effects.	temazepam, generic (15 mg) $22.22, (30 mg) $25.53; Restoril (15 mg) $65.04, (30 mg) $72.72
triazolam***	Halcion	0.125 to 0.5 mg at bedtime	Drowsiness, decreased muscle coordination, dizziness, lightheadedness, and amnesia are all possible side effects.	triazolam, generic (0.125 mg) $60.34; Halcion (0.125 mg) $63.65
buspirone	BuSpar	15 to 60 mg	This drug may cause dizziness, nausea, headache, nervousness, and lightheadedness. Unlike the benzodiazepines, it is non-addictive and non-sedating.	BuSpar (5 mg) $57.53
hydroxyzine	Atarax, Vistaril	50 to 200 mg	An antihistamine sometimes used to treat anxiety. May cause drowsiness and thickened mucus.	hydroxyzine, generic (25 mg) $9.74; Atarax (25 mg) $83.01; Vistaril (25 mg) $83.01
meprobamate	Miltown, Trancot	400 to 1,600 mg	Less effective than benzodiazepines. Drowsiness, unsteadiness, and confusion are possible side effects.	meprobamate, generic (200 mg) $4.61; Miltown (200 mg) $103.60; Trancot (200 mg) $2.10

*These dosages represent an average range for the treatment of anxiety. The precise effective dosage varies from patient to patient and depends on many factors. Do not make any changes in your medication without consulting your doctor.

**Average wholesale prices to pharmacists for 100 tablets or capsules of the dosage amount listed in parentheses. Costs to consumers are higher.

***Short- or intermediate-acting drug.

Source: *Red Book, 1995* (Medical Economics Data, publishers).

ous anxiety disorders respond differently to the types of treatments available, and, for a specific disorder, some treatments may be better than others.

Panic disorder. Treatment of panic disorder often involves both psychotherapy and pharmacologic measures. Referral to a therapist who is experienced in treating panic disorder is often necessary. Growing evidence suggests that cognitive and behavioral psychotherapy, based on graded exposure to situations that induce symptoms of anxiety, are effective treatments for panic disorder. The mainstay of pharmacologic treatment has been the tricyclic antidepressants or monoamine oxidase inhibitors, both of which are 80 to 90% effective in blocking panic attacks, but require 6 to 12 weeks to take effect. High doses of alprazolam, one of the newer benzodiazepines, can be effective within a few days and cause fewer side effects than the antidepressants. Nevertheless, like other benzodiazepines, alprazolam can be addicting. Beta blockers, such as propranolol or atenolol, can halt the physical symptoms of panic attacks, but do not prevent the fear or panic itself. A relapse of symptoms occurs in 30 to 60% of patients, 6 to 12 months after drugs are discontinued.

Generalized anxiety disorder. Despite its more chronic course, GAD is more responsive to treatment than panic disorder. Supportive and behavioral psychotherapy benefit many individuals. Persistent symptoms can lead to depression and abuse of alcohol and drugs—especially of benzodiazepines, the most common form of drug treatment for GAD. Treatment with benzodiazepines should be limited to short (five- to seven-day) courses to avoid dependence. Buspirone may become the first-choice drug in the future because it does not cause dependence or withdrawal symptoms.

A recent study found that over the long term, the antidepressant imipramine might be even more effective for GAD than benzodiazepines. In this study, 250 individuals who fit the criteria for GAD received either imipramine, trazodone (another antidepressant), diazepam (a benzodiazepine), or a placebo. Two weeks into the eight-week study, diazepam had the greatest anxiety-relieving effect. At the end of the study, however, those taking imipramine had significantly greater improvement than subjects taking trazodone, diazepam, or the placebo. Both antidepressants produced more adverse side effects than diazepam, but the same number of participants dropped out of the study with each drug tested. Imipramine had fewer side effects than trazodone. In addition, antidepressants do not carry the risk of dependence, and thus would

NEW RECOMMENDATION

Easing the Switch from Benzodiazepines

Although benzodiazepines are considered safe and effective, some patients may need to switch to another medication (due to lack of improvement or to side effects, for example). However, an abrupt switch may lead to withdrawal reactions or a return of anxiety symptoms. According to a recent study of 44 patients with generalized anxiety disorder, the transition can be eased by immediately starting on the new drug, while tapering off the old one. In the study, researchers randomly selected patients to receive either a placebo or buspirone (BuSpar) while their dosage of the benzodiazepine lorazepam (Alzapam) was gradually decreased over a two-week period.

Anxiety scores stayed the same or improved when buspirone was started as lorazepam was tapered off. Buspirone patients also experienced no benzodiazepine withdrawal symptoms and fewer side effects compared to the placebo group. As the study's authors conclude: "This indicates that buspirone may be useful if added during lorazepam tapering." This method can help to prevent patients from resuming use of benzodiazepines in order to avoid withdrawal and/or a return of anxiety.

JOURNAL OF CLINICAL PSYCHOPHARMACOLOGY
VOLUME 15, NUMBER 1
February 1995

be a safer choice for long-term use. While the results of this study need to be replicated in long-term trials, they point to a role for antidepressants in the treatment of GAD.

Cutting back on caffeine may also help ease the symptoms of GAD. One study compared the effects of 250 milligrams of caffeine, 500 milligrams of caffeine, and a placebo in 36 men and women—12 with GAD, 12 with panic disorder, and 12 with no history of psychiatric illness. Caffeine had an effect on physical measures of anxiety—such as blood pressure, pulse rate, and brain activity—in all participants, but the effects were strongest in those with GAD. In addition, more subjects with GAD reported heightened subjective symptoms of anxiety. Both the physical and subjective symptoms were dose-related—that is, the response to 500 milligrams of caffeine was greater than to 250 milligrams of caffeine. (If you decide to eliminate caffeine from your diet, cut back gradually, since stopping caffeine intake suddenly can produce withdrawal symptoms, such as severe headaches and nausea.)

Obsessive-compulsive disorder. As in the case of panic disorder, patients with OCD may benefit from cognitive and behavioral psychotherapy. An important recent pharmacologic advance is the effective use of serotonin reuptake inhibitors in treating this illness. Improvements, which may take six to eight weeks of drug therapy, are more likely for compulsions than obsessions.

Post-traumatic stress disorder. Successful treatment requires a combination of psychotherapy—aimed at desensitizing the individual to the traumatic experience—and medication. Amitriptyline and desipramine are commonly used to treat the mood disturbances and anxiety that accompany the disorder.

Phobias. When treatment is needed, behavioral psychotherapy may help desensitize the person to the thing or situation that causes the fear. The therapist can teach the patient to use relaxation techniques when confronted by fear. Beta blockers reduce the physical symptoms of performance anxiety, but may not decrease its psychological aspects.

HEALTH INFORMATION ORGANIZATIONS AND SUPPORT GROUPS

American Mental Health
Counselors Association
5999 Stevenson Ave.
Alexandria, VA 22304
800-326-2642/703-823-9800

American Psychiatric Association
1400 K Street NW
Washington, DC 20005
202-682-6000

American Psychological Association
750 First Street NE
Washington, DC 20002
202-336-5500

Council on Anxiety Disorders
PO Box 17011
Winston-Salem, NC 27116
910-722-7760

Depression and Related Affective
Disorders Association
Johns Hopkins Hospital
600 N. Wolfe Street
Meyer 3-181
Baltimore, MD 21205
410-955-4647

Depression Awareness Recognition
& Treatment Program
5600 Fishers Lane
Rm. 10-85, Parklawn Bldg.
Rockville, MD 20857
800-421-4211/301-443-4140

Emotional Health Anonymous
PO Box 429
Glendale, CA 91209
310-679-2671

Emotions Anonymous
PO Box 4245
St. Paul, MN 55104-0245
612-647-9712

National Alliance for the Mentally Ill
200 North Glebe Rd., Suite 1015
Arlington, VA 22203-3754
800-950-6264/703-524-7600

National Association of
Psychiatric Health Systems
1319 F Street N.W., Suite 1000
Washington, DC 20004
202-393-6700

National Depressive and
Manic-Depressive Association
730 N. Franklin, Suite 501
Chicago, IL 60610
312-642-0049

National Mental Health Association
1021 Prince Street
Alexandria, VA 22314-2971
703-684-7722

LEADING PSYCHIATRIC HOSPITALS

U.S. News & World Report and the National Opinion Research Center, a social-science research group at the University of Chicago, conduct a yearly survey of 2,400 physicians in 16 medical specialties. This year, the doctors were asked to nominate the five hospitals they consider best for their specialty from among 1,631 major academic institutions and specialized medical centers, ignoring location and expense. This is the current list of the best psychiatric hospitals for both inpatient and outpatient care, as determined by the doctors' recommendations from 1993, 1994, and 1995 and factual data regarding several quality indicators, such as the ratio of specialists to beds and the availability of post-discharge services. It is important to remember, however, that the methods used to conduct the survey are not foolproof, since the results reflect in part the doctors' subjective opinions. All listed institutions are considered leading centers, but the rankings do not imply that other hospitals cannot or do not deliver excellent care.

C. F. Menninger
Memorial Hospital
5800 S.W. Sixth St.
Topeka, KS 66606
913-273-7500

Massachusetts General Hospital
55 Fruit St.
Boston, MA 02114
617-726-2000

McLean Hospital
115 Mill St.
Belmont, MA 02178
617-855-2000

Johns Hopkins Hospital
600 N. Wolfe St.
Baltimore, MD 21287
410-955-5464

New York Hospital—
Cornell Medical Center
525 E. 68th St.
New York, NY 10021
212-746-5454

Mayo Clinic
200 S.W. First St.
Rochester, MN 55905
507-284-2511

Columbia-Presbyterian
Medical Center
622 West 168th St.
New York, NY 10032
212-305-2500

Sheppard and Enoch Pratt Hospital
6501 N. Charles St.
PO Box 6815
Baltimore, MD 21285-6815
410-938-3000

New York University Medical Center
560 1st Ave.
New York, NY 10016
212-263-7300

UCLA Neuropsychiatric Hospital
10833 LeConte Ave.
Los Angeles, CA 90095
310-825-9111

BIBLIOGRAPHY

This list contains some of the more important studies in depression and anxiety published this year.

Ball, S.G. et al. "Depression and Generalized Anxiety Symptoms in Panic Disorder: Implications for Comorbidity." *The Journal of Nervous and Mental Disease* 183 (May 1995): 304-308.

Chiaie, R.D. et al. "Assessment of the Efficacy of Buspirone in Patients Affected by Generalized Anxiety Disorder, Shifting to Buspirone from Prior Treatment with Lorazepam." *Journal of Clinical Psychopharmacology* 15 (February 1995): 12-19.

Cornelius, J.R. et al. "Disproportionate Suicidality in Patients with Comorbid Major Depression and Alcoholism." *American Journal of Psychiatry* 152 (March 1995): 358-364.

Coulter, D.M. and Pillans, P.I. "Fluoxetine and Extrapyramidal Side Effects." *American Journal of Psychiatry* 152 (January 1995): 122-124.

Food and Drug Administration. "Eldepryl and Antidepressant Interaction." *FDA Medical Bulletin (Drug Bulletin)* 25, February 1995.

Friedman, R.A. et al. "Retreatment for Relapse Following Desipramine Discontinuation in Dysthymia." *American Journal of Psychiatry* 152 (June 1995): 926-928.

George, M.S. et al. "Brain Activity During Transient Sadness and Happiness in Healthy Women." *American Journal of Psychiatry* 152 (March 1995): 341-351.

Greist, J. et al. "Double-Blind Parallel Comparison of Three Dosages of Sertraline and Placebo in Outpatients with Obsessive-Compulsive Disorder." *Archives of General Psychiatry* 52 (April 1995): 289-294.

Hays, R.D. et al. "Functioning and Well-being Outcomes of Patients with Depression Compared with Chronic General Mental Illness." *Archives of General Psychiatry* 52 (January 1995): 11-19.

Katon, W. et al. "Collaborative Management to Achieve Treatment Guidelines: Impact on Depression in Primary Care." *Journal of the American Medical Association* 273 (April 5, 1995): 1026-1031.

Keith, S.J. and Matthews, S.M. "The Value of Psychiatric Treatment: Its Efficacy in Severe Mental Disorders." *Psychopharmacology Bulletin* 29 (1993): 427-430.

Kendler, K.S. et al. "Stressful Life Events, Genetic Liability, and Onset of an Episode of Major Depression in Women." *American Journal of Psychiatry* 152 (June 1995): 833-842.

Kessler, R.C. et al. "Lifetime and 12-Month Prevalence of DSM-III-R Psychiatric Disorders in the United States: Results from the National Comorbidity Study." *Archives of General Psychiatry* 51 (January 1994): 8-19.

Krishnan, K.R.R. et al. "Clinical and Phenomenological Comparisons of Late-Onset and Early-Onset Depression." *American Journal of Psychiatry* 152 (May 1995): 785-788.

Lichtenberg, P.A. et al. "The Relationship Between Depression and Cognition in Older Adults: A Cross-validation Study." *Journal of Gerontology* 508 (January 1995): P25-P32.

Leon, A.C. et al. "The Social Costs of Anxiety Disorders." *British Journal of Psychiatry* 166 (April 1995): 19-22.

Martin, L.M. et al. "Recognition and Management of Anxiety and Depression in Elderly Patients." *Mayo Clinic Proceedings* 70 (October 1995): 999-1006.

Merikangas, K.R. and Angst, J. "Comorbidity and Social Phobia: Evidence from Clinical, Epidemiologic, and Genetic Studies." *European Archives of Psychiatry and Clinical Neuroscience* 244 (February 1995): 297-303.

Mirowsky, J. and Ross, C.E. "Sex Differences in Distress: Real or Artifact?" *American Sociological Review* 60 (June 1995): 449-468.

Mynors-Wallis, L.M. et al. "Randomised Controlled Trial Comparing Problem Solving Treatment with Amitriptyline and Placebo for Major Depression in Primary Care." *British Medical Journal* 310 (February 18, 1995): 441-445.

Radloff, L.S. "The CES-D Scale: A Self-Report Depression Scale for Research in the General Population." *Applied Psychological Measurement* 1 (1977): 385-401.

Schulberg, H.C. et al. "Applicability of Clinical Pharmacotherapy Guidelines for Major Depression in Primary Care Settings." *Archives of Family Medicine* 4 (February 1995): 106-112.

U.S. Department of Health and Human Services, Agency for Health Care Policy and Research. *Depression in Primary Care,* Volumes 1 and 2. Clinical Practice Guideline No. 5, April 1993.

This thorough discussion of the diagnosis and treatment of depression and anxiety will benefit persons of all ages. — THE EDITORS

mayo

Recognition and Management of Anxiety and Depression in Elderly Patients

LAWRENCE M. MARTIN, M.D., KEVIN C. FLEMING, M.D., AND JONATHAN M. EVANS, M.D.

• *Objective*: To describe important aspects of the recognition and management of anxiety and depression in elderly patients.

• *Design*: We reviewed pertinent recent articles in the medical literature and compiled guidelines for diagnosing and treating anxiety and depression in the geriatric population.

• *Results*: Depression and anxiety are common in the elderly population. The development of depression in elderly subjects is associated with a higher risk of death from suicide than for any other age-group. Recognition of depression in elderly patients is often hampered by an inability or reluctance on the part of these patients to report depressive symptoms. In addition, anxiety and depression are often attributed to organic illness in this age-group. Pharmacotherapy is effective; however, older patients are probably more likely than young patients to experience adverse effects. Using medications at lower doses, choosing drugs with shorter half-lives, and avoiding drugs with potent anticholinergic side effects are often advisable.

• *Conclusion*: Anxiety and depression are common conditions among the elderly population. Correct recognition, attention to underlying precipitating factors, and compassionate, supportive care can vastly improve the quality of the lives of these patients.

(*Mayo Clin Proc 1995; 70:999-1006*)

Thoughts about aging may induce anxiety. When a chronologic milestone is reached, we may describe ourselves as "depressed." These common reactions may be among the factors that complicate the recognition of anxiety and depressive syndromes in elderly patients. The fact that our culture perceives growing older as something to fear and avoid may diminish our sensitivity to treatable conditions in old age. Elderly patients themselves often assume that growing older is both frightening and depressing. Thus, they are reluctant to seek help for "normal" reactions.

If elderly patients request medical assistance because of anxiety and depression, the setting is likely to be the office of their primary physician rather than an outpatient psychiatric clinic. This pattern will become even more common in the era of managed care.

ANXIETY

Characteristic Features.—Anxiety can be defined as worry, apprehension, or panic that occurs in the absence of, or is out of proportion to, an actual threat. Usually, such reactions are associated with unpleasant autonomic nervous system arousal. Symptoms of sympathetic arousal such as tachycardia, tremor, hyperventilation, and light-headedness, as well as complaints of inner tremulousness and unsteadiness, are likely to prompt a patient with anxiety to consult a physician. Less common are complaints of "nerves" or fearfulness. True anxiety or panic episodes often precipitate visits to the emergency department, where electrocardiography, blood gas studies, and computed tomographic scanning are done to rule out acute cardiovascular or central nervous system disease.

Frequently, the outcome of these brief encounters is dissatisfying to both the patient and the physician. The physician, in a well-meaning attempt to reassure the frightened patient, relates that "nothing is wrong" or "it's just nerves." At times, a low-dose benzodiazepine is prescribed. The patient who has experienced a frightening constellation of physical symptoms tends to feel doubtful and embarrassed by the experience. The perception may be that if it is simply nerves, then perhaps it should be tolerated or overcome through willpower alone.

Although the reported prevalence of formal diagnoses of primary anxiety disorders in the elderly population is actually less than that in the general adult population,[1] the number of anxiety-related complaints encountered by primary physicians from patients in this age-group may not be decreased. In fact, the commonly diagnosed anxiety disorders (panic disorders, phobic illnesses, obsessive-compulsive disorder, posttraumatic stress disorder, and generalized anxiety disorder) may be only the tip of the symptomatic iceberg. Estimates of the prevalence of anxiety among elderly patients may be spuriously low because of lack of recognition or misdiagnosis as organic illness.

Moreover, numerous other psychiatric and medical conditions are increasingly associated with complaints of anxiety in elderly subjects (Table 1). To the array of other conditions that may manifest with symptoms of anxiety, one might add long-term, excessive social drug or substance use (such as caffeine, tobacco products, and chocolate).

Assessment.—The evaluation of anxiety should encompass a description of the current symptoms, previous episodes, other past psychiatric history, medical conditions, current and past medications, life or situational changes, and history of alcohol use. A physical examination should focus on the stigmas of the organic causes of anxiety. Laboratory screening to investigate suspected medical conditions might include serum electrolyte values, complete blood cell count, thyroid function studies, chest roentgenography, and electrocardiography. Specialized testing such as urine collection for metanephrines in patients with symptoms of anxiety and hypertension, computed tomography of the head, electroencephalography, or psychometric testing should be performed only in the presence of specific findings on the history, the physical examination, or the mental status examination.

With this approach, the examining physician is provided with considerable information about the likely origins of the symptoms of anxiety, and the distressed patient is reassured that symptoms are being thoroughly evaluated. If anxiety disorder is subsequently diagnosed, the somatically concerned patient may accept the diagnosis and treatment because of the meticulous assessment.

Further inquiry should be made into likely areas of situational stress, loss, or conflict. *Environmental stressors*, such as the lack of social networks, problems with housing, financial difficulties, and problems with mobility or transportation, can cause considerable concern. Such difficulties threaten the physical security and independence of a person. *Adaptational stressors* may include an experience of displacement or sudden loss such as a move to a nursing home or death of a spouse, retirement, or a major change in physical health.

Treatment.—Symptoms of anxiety are not always treated with antianxiety agents. Obvious examples in which antianxiety agents are relatively contraindicated can be found among the conditions listed in Table 1. Prescribing an agent that may sedate, compromise equilibrium, depress respiratory drive, or increase confusion has drawbacks in some of the common neurologic and medical illnesses encountered in the elderly population. Transient anxiety associated with life losses or changes may be another example. When a child is frightened or worried, we seldom respond by giving a pill. We hold the child, listen, and validate that the feelings are real and frightening and that they are normal to experience. A similar approach may be appropriate in elderly patients. The assurance that support is available, that abandonment will not ensue despite life changes or losses, and that symptoms or fears are real and normal may be a powerful anxiolytic. This response provides the foundation for competent and effective medical care for patients of all ages.

Table 1.—**Conditions Associated With Anxiety in Elderly Patients**

Axis I psychiatric syndromes, including major depression and senile dementia
Personality disorders
Alcoholism, benzodiazepine abuse and dependence
Chronic pain syndromes
Chronic insomnia
Transient anxiety associated with negative life events
Medical conditions (cardiovascular disease, chronic respiratory disease, Parkinson's disease, movement disorders, thyroid dysfunction)
Pharmacologic treatments (corticosteroids, theophylline, thyroid hormone, antipsychotic and antidepressant medications)

From Abrams.[1] By permission.

Specific behavioral management techniques, either alone or in conjunction with pharmacotherapy, have been shown to be effective for symptoms of anxiety. Physical therapy instruction in muscle relaxation techniques or referral to a psychologist for training in relaxation techniques or cognitive psychotherapy may enhance a personal sense of bodily control.

Psychotherapy provided by an empathetic, skilled, sanctioned professional often helps the patient who is suffering from situational anxiety to explore and understand fears. Such treatment may diminish the need for or the amount of pharmacologic intervention.

Despite these nonpharmacologic options, the most commonly prescribed treatment for anxiety-related symptoms in elderly patients is antianxiety medication. A 1983 survey of medication use by patients 60 to 74 years of age showed that 11% of men and 25% of women used anxiolytic drugs. This same survey noted that, at that time, the age-group beyond 65 years constituted 10% of the population but accounted for 21% of all prescriptions for diazepam.[1]

Although frequently prescribed, benzodiazepines can have serious side effects in the elderly population. All benzodiazepines have the potential to induce tolerance and thus be associated with breakthrough symptoms of anxiety and the need to increase the dose. Long-term use of these medications may increase central nervous system depression, confusion, ataxia, and falls in an already vulnerable population. Because the half-life of all medications, including benzodiazepines, can be substantially prolonged in elderly subjects, ongoing use necessitates careful, *regular* monitoring to avoid problems associated with accumulation in tissues. Explicit written and verbal instructions for proper use of medications are essential.

As with other types of medications, the best application of antianxiety pharmacotherapy is to familiarize oneself with a few medications in a specific class and become skilled with their use. No specific indications exist for use of benzodiazepines. Notably increased symptoms of anxiety that interfere with daily function or activities may be a reasonable hallmark for initiation of such therapy. Relative contraindications are chronic anxiety, potential danger from side effects (that is, sedation in someone who needs to be alert), chronic obstructive pulmonary disease, other sedative-hypnotic use, gait instability, and a past history of alcoholism or benzodiazepine dependence.

Long-acting benzodiazepines have the advantage of fewer peaks and valleys in blood level, which decreases the likelihood of recurrent anxiety between dosing. With these drugs, less frequent administration is possible, and tapering the dose or withdrawing therapy may be easier. The disadvantages of long-acting benzodiazepines are the potential for gradual accumulation because of generally slower metabolism and excretion in elderly patients and the unpredictable accumulation of metabolites with extremely long half-lives. Two commonly used long-acting benzodiazepines are diazepam and chlordiazepoxide. These drugs have no appreciable cardiovascular side effects but have an active metabolite (desmethyldiazepam) with a half-life of 50 to 100 hours in normal adults.[2] Although available in an injectable form, intramuscular injection for control of anxiety is not recommended. Because these medications are inconsistently absorbed from muscle tissue, the response may be unpredictable. Clonazepam is another frequently used long-acting benzodiazepine. This medication is generally administered twice a day and is available in extremely small dosages—0.5 mg, one-half to one tablet twice daily, may effectively relieve anxiety within a period of several days. The duration of time needed to achieve peak serum concentrations makes it less effective for acute anxiety. In occasional cases, the dosage can be increased to 1 or even 2 mg twice daily.

Short-acting benzodiazepines have several advantages over drugs with longer half-lives. They tend to have a very rapid response rate (within minutes), which may be beneficial in acute anxiety. The shorter half-lives and essentially no active metabolites result in less likelihood of long-term and inconsistent accumulation. The disadvantages of short-acting anxiolytics include a relative ineffectiveness for long-term management of anxiety. The most commonly used short-acting benzodiazepine is lorazepam. It has a short and predictable half-life and is available in small dosages. It is also the only benzodiazepine that is consistently absorbed when injected intramuscularly. This response allows rapid and safe tranquilization in emergent settings. The short half-life of lorazepam makes it ideal for situational anxiety settings; for example, it may be useful as a pretreatment in an anxious and demented patient before hands-on care such as bathing. It also may be used to target symptoms of anxiety that may occur at specific times of day.

The *atypical antianxiety agent* buspirone hydrochloride has proved useful in the treatment of chronic generalized anxiety disorder; it is less likely to be of benefit for treating acute anxiety situations or panic episodes. The advantages of buspirone are its relative safety, absence of interactions with other drugs, and unlikely induction of tolerance or dependence. This medication is prescribed beginning at low dosages (5 mg twice daily) and gradually increased as tolerated during a several-week span to a total of 30 to 40 mg daily in divided doses. A period of administration of 6 to 8 weeks is generally necessary for assessment of its efficacy.

Both *cyclic antidepressants* and *serotonin selective reuptake inhibitors* are effective for some types of anxiety. These medications should be considered for treatment of patients with panic episodes or concomitant depression because they are effective without the potential for habituation. They will be discussed in more detail in the subsequent section.

DEPRESSION

Many of the principles and caveats described in the previous section on anxiety are applicable for the recognition, evaluation, and treatment of depressive symptoms in older patients. Epidemiologic studies show that the incidence of *major depressive disorder* in late life is lower than in the general population.[3] Other studies, however, have reported an increase in *depressive symptoms* in this age-group.[4]

The diagnosis of both major depressive disorder and subsyndromal symptoms is complicated by difficulties that elderly patients may have in recognizing or describing depressive symptoms. These difficulties include a potential lack of knowledge or understanding of depression by both the patient and the caregivers; the tendency to avoid psychiatric care; a fear of expense for medical consultation; "aging" as a diagnosis and as a sufficient explanation for depressive symptoms for relatives, caregivers, and elderly patients themselves; and the absence of social or work contacts, which makes depressive symptoms more difficult to recognize and functional impairment more difficult to assess than in a younger age-group.

Table 2.—**Causes of Secondary Depression: Nonpsychiatric (Organic) Diseases**

Chronic infectious diseases
Hepatitis
Viral pneumonia
Mononucleosis
Tertiary syphilis
Other
Endocrinopathies
Hyperthyroidism
Hypothyroidism
Cushing's syndrome
Addison's disease
Hyperparathyroidism
Other
Malignant lesions
Pancreatic carcinoma
Uterine carcinoma
Other
Neurologic disorders
Epilepsy
Tumor
Huntington's disease
Parkinson's disease
Other (multiple sclerosis)
Hematologic disorders
Anemia (for example, pernicious anemia)
Major organ failure
Congestive heart failure
Pulmonary disease
Renal failure

From Finlayson and Martin.[5]

The physician's assessment of depression may be more complicated in the elderly population than in younger patients. A detailed history may be difficult to elicit because of cognitive impairment, reluctance, or denial by the patient or other history providers. Family members may be unavailable or overprotective. Geriatric patients have an increased likelihood of coexisting medical conditions, which may mimic or mask depressive illness (Table 2).[5] Depression may also manifest somewhat differently in elderly than in young patients. Some studies suggest that elderly patients may not express as many feelings of guilt and self-reproach but may be more somatically preoccupied than younger patients with major depression. Other conditions may make core depressive symptoms difficult to evaluate (for example, an elderly gentleman with ill-fitting dentures who lives alone may have other reasons for weight loss than the anorexia associated with depression).

Despite these complications, thorough elicitation of the history from the patient and family members is likely to provide a high index of suspicion of an underlying depressive disorder. A rapid change in personality, mentation, or level of function is illness, not aging. Often, depression is not the chief complaint in a patient who has a major depressive disorder. Despite some changes as previously noted, the classic symptoms (Table 3) tend to be common across the span of ages.

Often, a constellation of symptoms has been present in increasing severity for several weeks to months before medical assistance is sought. Despite the level of "depression," most major depressive symptoms in older patients tend to be physical in nature rather than related to mood. Some patients with classic depressive symptoms will deny any mood component to their illness.

Stroke is a special predisposing factor for depression in the elderly population. Impairment of speech or mentation may make interviewing the patient difficult. The patient, family, and care providers may assume that depressive symptoms are a normal response to the losses of function associated with the event. Nevertheless, depression after stroke often responds well to pharmacologic treatment if it is identified. Other common conditions that are associated with a high incidence of depression include dementia, myocardial infarction, coronary artery bypass grafting, and terminal illnesses. Untreated depression may slow the recovery or increase the debility and functional impairment associated with the primary condition.

Assessment.—Assessment of the depressed elderly patient is similar to that described earlier in this report for the elderly patient with anxiety. Of importance, outside information should be obtained from a friend or relative to corroborate or clarify symptom patterns, time of onset, baseline level of function, potential external life stressors, and possible use of alcohol or nonprescribed drugs. A detailed history of medical problems and current medications is important as well. Numerous other conditions must be considered in the differential diagnosis of depression. In addition

Table 3.—**Primary Major Depressive Symptoms**

Anhedonia (loss of ability to experience pleasure or look forward to previously enjoyed activities)
Agitation or psychomotor retardation
Anorexia and weight loss
Profound and unremitting fatigue
Loss of motivation or drive
Problems with concentration
Feelings of helplessness or being a burden
Hopelessness
Previous personal or family history of depression
Hypersomnia or insomnia
New delusional thinking, including somatic, guilt, or paranoid delusions

Table 4.—**Comparison of Pseudodementia and Dementia**

Characteristic	Pseudodementia	Dementia
Similarities		
Self-care	Lacking	Lacking
Restlessness	Present	Present
Irritability	Yes	Yes
Creativity	Absent	Absent
Somatic complaints	Yes	Yes
Orientation	Disturbed	Disturbed
Memory and concentration difficulties	Yes	Yes
Differences		
Onset	Quite abrupt	Insidious
Progression	Usually rapid	Usually slow
Patient awareness	Aware of deficits	Not as aware
Memory loss	Patient complains about it	Patient hides it (confabulates)
Responses	Global ("I don't know")	Near-miss answers
Patient emphasis	Deficits	Accomplishments
Nocturnal worsening	No	Usually
Mood	Depressed	Typically "happy"
Symptoms	Vegetative*	Nonvegetative
History of psychiatric disturbance	Common	Not common
Suicide risk	Considerable	Much lower

*Sleep disturbance, anorexia, fatigue, loss of sex drive.
Modified from Finlayson and Martin.[5]

to those listed in Table 2, the clinician should consider the initial manifestations of dementia, stroke, thyroid dysfunction, kidney failure, Parkinson's disease, viral encephalitis, brain tumor (particularly frontal or nondominant), undiagnosed and denied alcoholism, cancer of the lung or pancreas, pernicious anemia or folate deficiency, or an undiagnosed sleep disorder. Antipsychotic medication, frequently prescribed for agitation in demented persons, may cause blunted expression and psychomotor slowing that mimic depressive illness. The laboratory evaluation of first-time depression in an elderly patient should be dictated by clinical symptoms and abnormal physical findings.

A detailed history can also assist in distinguishing the thinking and behavioral changes associated with depression from those of a dementing illness. Some of the characteristic features of primary dementing illness and so-called pseudodementia (depression manifesting primarily as cognitive impairment) are compared in Table 4.[5] Many patients with a pseudodementia may have some elements of senile dementia remaining after depression has been treated.

Treatment.—Outcome studies of treatment of depression in elderly patients have shown varied results. Blazer[4] noted similar recovery from major depressive episodes in middle-aged and elderly adults. Patients at high risk for relapse or chronicity of depression were those with associated chronic health problems and poor social support systems.

General Guidelines.—The following is a recommended general approach to treatment of the elderly patient with depression: (1) correct any underlying organic illness that may be contributing; (2) minimize the use of depression-inducing medications, such as sedative-hypnotics, cimetidine, lipid-soluble β-blockers, or corticosteroids, when possible; (3) evaluate, correct, or attempt to alleviate the functional isolation and diminished independence caused by sensory deprivation or immobility; (4) increase stimulation in the living environment; (5) consider psychotherapeutic options, including referral for cognitive or supportive psychotherapy (group therapy is of particular benefit for those patients whose depressive symptoms are associated with specific losses or life changes); (6) in severe depression (associated with suicidal thinking, psychosis, or notable interference with daily activities or self-care), obtain a psychiatric consultation; and (7) consider pharmacotherapy. The clinician will frequently need to use several of these steps, either sequentially or in combination, to maximize the therapeutic response.

Antidepressants.—Antidepressants have become the most commonly prescribed of the psychotropic agents, supplanting antianxiety agents. Despite the increasing numbers and types of antidepressants, no individual agent has proved superior in efficacy. The choice of a specific antidepressant is therefore based on symptoms and side effects. Both antidepressant half-life and neurotransmitter uptake blockade vary considerably. The most common side effects are related to blockade of histamine H_1, muscarinic, acetylcholine, α_1-adrenergic, and dopamine D_2 receptors. The half-lives of the common cyclic antidepressants and serotonin selective reuptake inhibitors are compared in Figure 1.[6]

The potential side effects of the common antidepressants vary from helpful (sedation for the insomnia that accompanies depression) to irritating (dry mouth and constipation) to potentially dangerous (interactions with monoamine oxidase inhibitors, cardiac arrhythmias, and postural hypotension). Common side effects associated with neurotransmitter uptake and receptor site blockade are summarized in Table 5.[6]

The cyclic antidepressants, which have several advantages, have a proven track record of efficacy dating back to the 1950s. Many of these medications cause sedation, which can be beneficial for patients with insomnia associated with depression. Because several of these medications are available in a generic form, they may be less expensive than other drugs. The cyclic antidepressants have been used more frequently and have been studied more extensively in the treatment of pain problems. Serum blood levels are available for many of these medications, and some (nortriptyline and desipramine) have been standardized to provide therapeutic ranges.

The disadvantages of cyclic antidepressants in the elderly population include potential lethality and difficult treatment if the patient takes an overdose of these medications. Cardiotoxicity in association with delayed cardiac conduction and the potential to cause complete heart block in patients with conduction system disease may make these drugs dangerous to use. Common side effects are often unpleasant and, at times, make administration impossible, particularly in elderly patients. The anticholinergic side effects of these medications can increase confusion in the already cognitively impaired, depressed person. Postural hypotension, urinary retention, and constipation can be potentially dangerous side effects that are commonly reported.

Despite these potential drawbacks, age alone is no contraindication to judicious use. Commonly prescribed medications in this group include nortriptyline, desipramine, doxepin, and trazodone. Nortriptyline and desipramine are secondary amines and have fewer anticholinergic and antimuscarinic side effects than the tertiary amines, such as amitriptyline and imipramine. Peak serum concentrations are achieved in 4 to 8 hours for a secondary amine and 1 to 3 hours for a single dose of a tertiary amine. These qualities contribute to diminished bothersome (anticholinergic) and threatening (arrhythmia) side effects for the secondary amines.[7] The secondary amines are available in small doses; thus, cautious upward titration is possible. Medication is usually prescribed at bedtime, beginning with 10 mg and increasing by 10 mg once every week to 10 days as tolerated. Doxepin has a sedative effect and is available in small doses. This medication has pronounced anticholinergic effects and should be used with caution but can be well tolerated by some patients. Trazodone is the safest cyclic antidepressant in patients with cardiac conduction problems and glaucoma. It combines relatively safely with other classes of antidepressants, including monoamine oxidase inhibitors and serotonin reuptake blocking agents. It has a strong sedating side effect but little antimuscarinic effect; hence, it is relatively effective and safe for assisting with sleep without use of a benzodiazepine. If this medication is to be used independently as an antidepressant, twice-daily dosing is necessary—which may cause unacceptable amounts of postural hypotension and daytime sedation. It is frequently used in low doses as adjunctive treatment to assist with sleep at night. The suggested dose of trazodone for this purpose is 25 to 50 mg at bedtime.

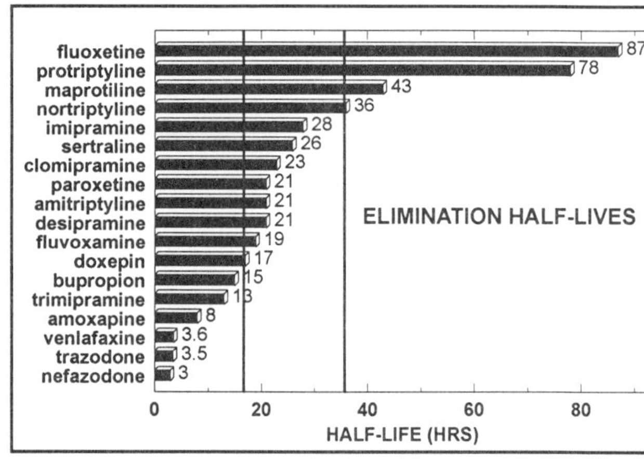

Fig. 1. Half-lives of common antidepressants. (From Richelson.[6])

The second commonly used class of antidepressant drugs are the serotonin reuptake inhibiting agents. These are the so-called new-generation antidepressants, of which fluoxetine (Prozac) was the original drug marketed in the United States. The advantages of these medications are primarily their safety and side-effect profile, and many physicians are comfortable prescribing them. Patients frequently tolerate them well without experiencing major side effects. These medications have minimal cardiovascular toxicity, and they have a low lethality in overdose. Most treated patients do not complain of sedation or constipation.

These medications are not without disadvantages, however. Their efficacy in major depressive disorders in comparison with the cyclic antidepressants is controversial. Blood levels are not readily available, nor are they particularly meaningful in regular clinical management at this time.

Common side effects may include anxiety, insomnia, nausea, and diarrhea; mild generalized headache is also frequently reported. Low-grade side effects seem to resolve and are not a source of ongoing difficulty for most patients. Sexual dysfunction, most commonly anorgasmy or delayed ejaculation, is frequently reported. Occasionally, a patient will be intolerant because of diarrhea or anxiety. These medications have not proved as effective for pain problems as the cyclic antidepressants. Fluoxetine has a lengthy half-life (87 hours) and an active metabolite with a half-life of 7 to 15 *days*.[6] Both fluoxetine and paroxetine may substantially increase serum levels of certain other medications by competing for and blocking cytochrome P_{450} oxidase 2D6 enzyme activity.[7] Potential interactions include monoamine oxidase inhibitors (contraindicated), cyclic antidepressants, orally administered anticoagulants, and hypoglycemic agents (insulin and oral).[8]

None of these medications has a clear-cut advantage over another for clinical care. Some clinicians may choose medications other than fluoxetine because of its long half-life and the need for close surveillance for interactions with other drugs. A reasonable treatment approach for a depressive illness in an elderly patient is administration of 25 mg of sertraline in the morning with breakfast for approximately 5 days to monitor for side effects, followed by an increase to 50 mg for 2 to 3 weeks. If the response is only partial but the medication is tolerated, further 50-mg increases to 150 mg would be indicated. Several new-generation antidepressants are available, and others are being introduced. The advantages touted are less for specific efficacy (with the exception of the obsessive-compulsive treatment qualities of fluvoxamine) than for having fewer serotonin selective reuptake inhibitor-type side effects.

Among the other categories of antidepressant and mood-stabilization medications are the monoamine oxidase inhibitors, psychostimulants, and mood-stabilizing drugs (commonly used for bipolar illness and including lithium, carbamazepine, and valproic acid). All these medications have their place in the treatment of mood disorders whether patients are young or old; however, they are seldom first-line medications because of the complexity of usage. These factors include the dietary restrictions and the major medication interactive potential of monoamine oxidase inhibitors and the need for frequent monitoring of laboratory determinations for the mood-stabilizing medications. Consequently, these medications are generally best used under the supervision of a psychiatrist.

Table 5.—**Pharmacologic Properties of Antidepressants and Their Possible Clinical Consequences**

Property	Possible clinical consequences
Blockade of norepinephrine uptake at nerve endings	Tremors Tachycardia Erectile and ejaculatory dysfunction Blockade of the antihypertensive effects of guanethidine and guanadrel Augmentation of pressor effects of sympathomimetic amines
Blockade of serotonin uptake at nerve endings	Gastrointestinal disturbances Increase or decrease in anxiety (dose-dependent) Sexual dysfunction Extrapyramidal side effects Interactions with L-tryptophan, monoamine oxidase inhibitors, and fenfluramine
Blockade of dopamine uptake at nerve endings	Psychomotor activation Antiparkinsonian effect Aggravation of psychosis
Blockade of histamine H_1 receptors	Potentiation of central depressant drugs Sedation, drowsiness Weight gain Hypotension
Blockade of muscarinic receptors	Blurred vision Dry mouth Sinus tachycardia Constipation Urinary retention Memory dysfunction
Blockade of α_1-adrenergic receptors	Potentiation of the antihypertensive effect of prazosin, terazosin, doxazosin, and labetalol Postural hypotension, dizziness Reflex tachycardia
Blockade of dopamine D_2 receptors	Extrapyramidal movement disorders Endocrine changes Sexual dysfunction (males)

From Richelson.[6]

SUICIDE

The need for all clinicians to consider and assess the possibly depressed patient for suicidal tendencies is not only appropriate medical practice but also the standard approach. The incidence of successful suicide increases steadily throughout the life span. The highest incidence of successful suicide is among white men older than 85 years of age. Persons who live alone and have a history of alcohol abuse and life losses, including major health changes, tend to be at even higher risk than the population as a whole. Do not be afraid to inquire of your patients: "Have you felt so low lately that life just doesn't seem worth living anymore?" or "Have you ever had suicidal thoughts?" If your patient responds affirmatively, further inquiry into a specific plan or preparations is appropriate. A psychiatric consultation for a complete assessment of active risk and treatment options should be obtained.

PSYCHIATRIC CONSULTATION

Obtaining a psychiatric consultation to assist in the initial assessment or management of the patient with depression or anxiety is always a consideration. Recent information has suggested that early involvement of psychiatrists and other mental health professionals improves outcomes and seems cost-effective.[9] If a person endorses suicidal thinking, further evaluation is imperative to assess the safety of outpatient treatment. Appreciable impairment in activities of daily living, including decision-making, nutrition, or self-care, may justify psychiatric consultation. The presence of psychosis accompanying depressive symptoms always warrants a psychiatric evaluation. A lack of response to initial therapeutic approaches should also prompt psychiatric assistance.

EDUCATION

Education is one of the most commonly overlooked components of the treatment of anxiety and depression in older persons. Busy physicians may think that they have neither the time nor the expertise to explain the likely diagnosis and the rationale for treatment. Moreover, the anxious, confused, or preoccupied patient may hear little of such an explanation. Although these observations may be true for patients of any age and with any illness, a diagnosis of a "mental" illness in an older patient often evokes negative, long-held views of a psychiatric problem as a character or coping weakness, rather than an illness. Thus, such a diagnosis may prompt a denial response that affects the patient's cooperation with treatment. Education in the form of discussion with the patient and family (with the patient's permission) and in the form of educational pamphlets to be read later may be of assistance in gaining the patient's understanding, acceptance, and active participation in the treatment of these conditions.

CONCLUSION

Elderly persons suffer from anxiety and depressive symptoms in response to various social, economic, medical, and personal losses and changes. Somatic complaints are common and may be the principal manifestation of the underlying disorder of mood and thinking. Primary-care physicians who are sensitive to these symptoms are likely to provide life-enhancing and perhaps lifesaving treatment for affected patients.

REFERENCES

1. Abrams R. Anxiety and personality disorders. In: Sadavoy J, Lazarus LW, Jarvik LF, editors. Comprehensive Review of Geriatric Psychiatry. Washington (DC): American Psychiatric Press, 1991: 369-386
2. Mayo Medical Center Drug Formulary 1994-1995. Hudson (OH): Lexi-Comp Inc., 1995: 209
3. Koenig HG, Blazer DG. Mood disorders and suicide. In: Birren JE, Sloane RB, Cohen GD, editors. Handbook of Mental Health and Aging. 2nd ed. San Diego: Academic Press, 1992: 383-384
4. Blazer DG. Affective disorders in late life. In: Busse EW, Blazer DG, editors. Geriatric Psychiatry. Washington (DC): American Psychiatric Press, 1989: 370-373
5. Finlayson RE, Martin LM. Recognition and management of depression in the elderly. Mayo Clin Proc 1982; 57:115-120
6. Richelson E. Pharmacology of antidepressants—characteristics of the ideal drug. Mayo Clin Proc 1994; 69:1069-1081
7. Preskorn SH. Pharmacokinetics of antidepressants: why and how they are relevant to treatment. J Clin Psychiatry 1993; 54(Suppl):14-34
8. PDR Guide to Drug Interactions, Side Effects, Indications [computer program]. Release 3.1. Montvale (NJ): Medical Economics Data Production Company, May 1991: 902
9. Sturm R, Wells KB. How can care for depression become more cost effective? JAMA 1995; 273:51-58

ISBN 0-929661-17-6
Third Printing

Printed in the United States of America

Medical Illustrator: Robert Duckwall, Johns Hopkins Medical School